MINISTER'S MANUAL

Compiled and Edited by
WILLIAM E. PICKTHORN

Volume 1
SERVICES FOR SPECIAL OCCASIONS

Volume 2
SERVICES FOR WEDDINGS
AND FUNERALS

Volume 3
SERVICES FOR MINISTERS
AND WORKERS

MINISTER'S MANUAL

MINISTER'S MANUAL

Compiled and Edited by
WILLIAM E. PICKTHORN

Volume 2

SERVICES FOR WEDDINGS AND FUNERALS

GOSPEL PUBLISHING HOUSE
Springfield, Missouri 65802

02-0548

13th Printing 2006

Library of Congress Catalog Card Number 65-13222
International Standard Book Number 0-88243-548-5

Printed in the United States of America

PREFACE

"It hardly needs to be said that set forms of devotion are uncongenial to those who practice a simple mode of worship and who stress spiritual liberty in prayer and preaching.

"Yet, while recognizing this fact it still remains true that there are special occasions where an appointed order is necessary for a well-conducted service. And if this is so, why be content with forms that are crude or badly prepared? Jesus in the Scripture portion known as the Lord's Prayer instructed the disciples: 'When ye pray, say . . .' The prophet Hosea once said to his countrymen: 'Take with you words, and turn to the Lord, and say to Him . . .' Hosea 14:2.

"There need be no morbid fear of lifeless ritual. As long as the spiritual vitality of the church is maintained the use of necessary forms will never become merely formal."

So wrote Myer Pearlman in the foreword to the first minister's manual produced by the Gospel Publishing House, *The Minister's Service Book*. These words, so true then, are just as true today. Every service must be ordered in some way, but no service need be lifeless and mechanical. The minister, guided by the Spirit, can select ceremonies which he feels contain the touch of the Spirit and which are appropriate to an occasion. Under the leading of the Spirit, he may adapt ceremonies to take into account unique circumstances. Perhaps he may even accept the challenge to write a ceremony of his own! Let this manual be a servant, not a master.

WILLIAM E. PICKTHORN
Christian Center
Palo Alto, California

ACKNOWLEDGMENTS

Credit for suggestions as to what should go into this volume is due to a great many ministers whose names are not in this book. They are men who wrote to say what they would like to see included even though they did not, themselves, submit forms for publication.

Credit for inspiration is due to a great many manuals published over a period of almost 90 years and by many different religious denominations. It is not thought that any of the material in this book has been lifted directly from any other manual. Forms sent by ministers who have contributed to the contents of this book were checked against the available manuals to avoid unintentional infringement of copyright. In instances where there were gaps in the materials received, the editor of this manual made outline notes on procedures detailed in various manuals, and, during a period of more than a year, revised the notes three or more times without reference to original sources so that the materials would become more and more his own. If there are forms in this manual resembling those of any other published book it is through sheer coincidence that they possess such similarity. On the other hand, where materials known to be in copyright have been included—as in the case of some hymns and special statements—permission for their use has been obtained from the copyright owners, and such use is acknowledged at appropriate points in the text.

Deep appreciation and fervent thanks are both extended to those who, through the years, have compiled such manuals. May their inspiration continue to affect others as it has me.

W.E.P.

CONTENTS

WEDDINGS

FUNERALS

Contents

Weddings

BIBLE REFERENCES

"And God said, Let us make man in our image, after our likeness: and let them have dominion over the fish of the sea, and over the fowl of the air, and over the cattle, and over all the earth, and over every creeping thing that creepeth upon the earth. So God created man in his own image, in the image of God created he him; male and female created he them." (Gen. 1:26, 27)

"And the Lord God said, It is not good that the man should be alone; I will make him an help meet for him." (Gen. 2:18)

"Therefore shall a man leave his father and his mother, and shall cleave unto his wife: and they shall be one flesh." (Gen. 2:24)

"And they called Rebekah, and said unto her, Wilt thou go with this man? And she said, I will go. And they sent away Rebekah their sister, and her nurse, and Abraham's servant, and his men. And they blessed Rebekah, and said unto her, Thou art our sister, be thou the mother of thousands of millions, and let thy seed possess the gate of those which hate them. And Rebekah arose, and her damsels, and they rode upon the camels, and followed the man: and the servant took Rebekah, and went his way. And Isaac came from the way of the well Lahairoi; for he dwelt in the south country. And Isaac went out to meditate in the field at eventide: and he lifted up his eyes, and saw, and, behold, the camels were coming. And Rebekah lifted up her eyes, and when she saw Isaac, she lighted off the camel. For she had said unto the servant, What man is this that walketh in the field to meet us? And the servant had said, It is my master: therefore she took a vail, and covered herself. And the servant told Isaac all things that he had done. And Isaac brought her into his mother Sarah's tent, and took Rebekah, and she became his wife; and he loved her." (Gen. 24:58-67)

"And Jacob loved Rachel; and said, I will serve thee seven years for Rachel thy younger daughter. And Jacob served seven years for Rachel; and they seemed unto him but a few days, for the love he had to her." (Gen. 29:18, 20)

"And David sent and communed with Abigail, to take her to him to wife. And when the servants of David were come to Abigail to Carmel, they spake unto her, saying, David sent us unto thee, to take thee to him to wife. And she arose, and bowed herself on her face to the earth, and said, Behold, let thine handmaid be a servant to wash the feet of the servants of my lord. And Abigail hasted, and arose, and rode upon an ass, with five damsels of her's that went after her; and she went after the messengers of David, and became his wife."

(1 Sam. 25:39-42)

"Hearken, O daughter, and consider, and incline thine ear; forget also thine own people, and thy father's house; so shall the king greatly desire thy

2

beauty: for he is thy Lord; and worship thou him. And the daughter of Tyre shall be there with a gift; even the rich among the people shall intreat thy favour. The king's daughter is all glorious within: her clothing is of wrought gold. She shall be brought unto the king in raiment of needlework: the virgins her companions that follow her shall be brought unto thee. With gladness and rejoicing shall they be brought: they shall enter into the king's palace."
(Ps. 45:10-15)

"Whoso findeth a wife findeth a good thing, and obtaineth favour of the Lord."   (Prov. 18:22)

"A prudent wife is from the Lord."   (Prov. 19:14)

"The Pharisees also came unto him, tempting him, and saying unto him, Is it lawful for a man to put away his wife for every cause? And he answered and said unto them, Have ye not read, that he which made them at the beginning made them male and female, and said, For this cause shall a man leave father and mother, and shall cleave to his wife: and they twain shall be one flesh? Wherefore they are no more twain, but one flesh. What therefore God hath joined together, let not man put asunder. They say unto him, Why did Moses then command to give a writing of divorcement, and to put her away? He saith unto them, Moses because of the hardness of your hearts suffered you to put away your wives: but from the beginning it was not so. And I say unto you, Whosoever shall put away his wife, except

3

it be for fornication, and shall marry another, committeth adultery: and whoso marrieth her which is put away doth commit adultery." (Matt. 19:3-9)

"And the third day there was a marriage in Cana of Galilee; and the mother of Jesus was there: and both Jesus was called, and his disciples, to the marriage." (John 2:1, 2)

"Know ye not, brethren, (for I speak to them that know the law,) how that the law hath dominion over a man as long as he liveth? For the woman which hath an husband is bound by the law to her husband so long as he liveth; but if the husband be dead, she is loosed from the law of her husband. So then if, while her husband liveth, she be married to another man, she shall be called an adulteress: but if her husband be dead, she is free from that law; so that she is no adulteress, though she be married to another man." (Rom. 7:1-3)

"Let the husband render unto the wife due benevolence: and likewise also the wife unto the husband. The wife hath not power of her own body, but the husband: and likewise also the husband hath not power of his own body, but the wife."

(1 Cor. 7:3, 4)

"Wives, submit yourselves unto your own husbands, as unto the Lord. For the husband is the head of the wife, even as Christ is the head of the church: and he is the saviour of the body. Therefore as the church is subject unto Christ, so let the wives

4

be to their own husbands in every thing. Husbands, love your wives, even as Christ also loved the church, and gave himself for it; that he might sanctify and cleanse it with the washing of water by the word, that he might present it to himself a glorious church, not having spot, or wrinkle, or any such thing; but that it should be holy and without blemish. So ought men to love their wives as their own bodies. He that loveth his wife loveth himself. For no man ever yet hated his own flesh; but nourisheth and cherisheth it, even as the Lord the church: for we are members of his body, of his flesh, and of his bones. For this cause shall a man leave his father and mother, and shall be joined unto his wife, and they two shall be one flesh. This is a great mystery: but I speak concerning Christ and the church. Nevertheless let every one of you in particular so love his wife even as himself; and the wife see that she reverence her husband." (Eph. 5:22-33)

"Husbands, love your wives, even as Christ also loved the church, and gave himself for it."
(Eph. 5:25)

"Marriage is honourable in all, and the bed undefiled: but whoremongers and adulterers God will judge." (Heb. 13:4)

"Wives, be in subjection to your own husbands; that, if any obey not the word, they also may without the word be won by the conversation of the wives; while they behold your chaste conversation coupled with fear. Whose adorning let it not be that outward adorning of plaiting the hair, and of wearing of gold, or of putting on of apparel; but let it be the hidden man of the heart, in that which is not corruptible, even the ornament of a meek and quiet spirit, which is in the sight of God of great price. For after this manner in the old time the holy women also, who trusted in God, adorned themselves, being in subjection unto their own husbands: even as Sara obeyed Abraham, calling him lord: whose daughters ye are, as long as ye do well, and are not afraid with any amazement. Likewise, ye husbands, dwell with them according to knowledge, giving honour unto the wife, as unto the weaker vessel, and as being heirs together of the grace of life; that your prayers be not hindered." (1 Peter 3:1-7)

"Let us be glad and rejoice, and give honour to him: for the marriage of the Lamb is come, and his wife hath made herself ready. And to her was granted that she should be arrayed in fine linen, clean and white: for the fine linen is the righteousness of saints. And he saith unto me, Write, Blessed are they which are called unto the marriage supper of the Lamb." (Rev. 19:7-9)

ADDRESS

The parties shall stand before the minister, the man on the right and the woman on the left; and the minister may say to the assembled guests:

Of the world's three great institutions—the home, the church, and the state—the home is the oldest and most sacred.

In the consummation of the first marriage, the woman whom God made as a helpmeet for man was not taken from his head to rule over him, nor from his feet to be trampled by him, but from his side that she might be his equal, from under his arm that she might receive his protection, and from near his heart that she might own and command his love.

The relation of husband and wife is most sacred when it is that of "two souls with a single thought . . . two hearts that beat as one." It is the blending of two lives, the union of two natures.

GIVING THE BRIDE

The minister shall then ask:
Who giveth this woman to be married to this man?
The father of the bride shall answer:
Her mother and I.

ADDRESS TO THE GROOM

The minister shall address the groom by name, saying:
———— (name), you are about to take upon

yourself a pure resolve, a solemn vow, incurring grave and lasting responsibilities. The woman of your choice is now to become the partner of your life, the coheir of your possessions, the queen of your home. In no other way could she so manifest her love for you. She leaves her home ties, the companionship of friends—all these—to share with you the joys and sorrows of life. With you will she now abide, and for you will she live.

ADDRESS TO THE BRIDE

In like manner the minister shall address the bride:

——— (name), you are also to assume grave responsibilities. He whom you are about to wed will look to you for solace in the hour of trial. Your smile should be his brightest day, your voice his sweetest music, your industry his greatest wealth, your economy his safest steward, your lips his faithful counsellor, and your prayers his most able advocate at heaven's court.

VOWS

Addressing the groom, the minister shall ask:

——— (man), do you take——— (woman), in the presence of these witnesses and according to the laws of this state, to be your lawfully wedded wife?

The man shall answer:

I do.

Addressing the bride, the minister shall ask:

————— (woman), do you take————— (man), in the presence of these witnesses and according to the laws of this state, to be your lawfully wedded husband?

The woman shall answer:

I do.

THE TOKEN

The minister shall ask:

Do you have a ring (rings) with which to seal these marriage vows?

The bride's ring shall be given to the minister who shall hand it to the groom and instruct him to place it on the fourth finger of the bride's left hand and repeat after him:

————— (woman), with this ring I thee wed, and with all my worldly goods I thee endow, in the name of the Father, and of the Son, and of the Holy Spirit.

If there is a second ring it shall be given to the minister who shall hand it to the bride and instruct her to place it on the fourth finger of the groom's left hand and repeat after him:

————— (man), with this ·ring I thee wed, and to thee my love I pledge, in the name of the Father, and of the Son, and of the Holy Spirit.

PRONOUNCEMENT

The couple shall be instructed to join right hands. Then the minister shall say:

With this union of hearts and hands, and by

the authority vested in me as a minister of the gospel, and by the laws of the State of————, and in the name of Almighty God, our Father, I pronounce you man and wife.

PRAYER

The couple shall kneel as the minister prays for God's blessing and guidance in their lives together.

BENEDICTION

And now, "may the Lord bless thee and keep thee, the Lord make His face to shine upon thee, and be gracious unto thee: the Lord lift up His countenance upon thee and give thee peace." In Christ's name. Amen.

—An old ceremony handed down in the family of the minister who originated it.

Submitted by *J. C. Tinsman*

WEDDING CEREMONY

ADDRESS TO THE GUESTS

Addressing the assembled guests, the minister may say:

When God wished to describe the beauty and unity and completeness of the Church, when God wished to reveal to mortal understanding the happy estate of His people, He chose to picture a wedding— a devoted bridegroom with his spotless, glowing bride.

We have gathered to share in the joy of these who have come to join themselves as God's perfect type of everlasting love. We have gathered here to wish for them a union which shall rejoice the heart of God and make His picture true before mankind.

ADDRESS TO THE PARTIES

To the parties who have come to be married, the minister may say:

This marriage in which you come to be united is a holy ordinance, instituted by God at creation, honored by Jesus Christ at the wedding in Cana, and commended by the Holy Spirit as evidenced in the writings of the Apostle Paul.

In making the marriage union a type of Christ and His Church, God has made known to you the tenderness with which He looks upon this moment. He has made you aware of your blessings and your obligations to Him and to one another. He has spoken the substance of the marriage laws: "Let the wife reverence her husband. . . . Husbands love your wives even as Christ also loved the church and gave himself for it."

Addressing the man, the minister shall ask:

Having a full understanding of the privileges and obligations of this Christian marriage, will you take this woman to be your wife, to live together in the holy estate of matrimony, to love and to cherish as long as you both shall live?

The man shall answer:

I will.

Addressing the woman, the minister shall ask:

Having a full understanding of the privileges and obligations of this Christian marriage, will you take this man to be your husband, to live together in the holy estate of matrimony, to love and to cherish as long as you both shall live?

The woman shall answer:

I will.

GIVING THE BRIDE

The minister shall ask the father of the bride:

Who gives this woman to be married to this man?

The father shall answer:

I do.

VOWS

The man and the woman shall be instructed to join right hands. Then the man shall repeat after the minister:

I,————— (man), take you,————— (woman), to

be my wife, according to the ordinances of God, to love and to cherish as long as we both shall live.

In the same manner, the woman shall repeat after the minister:

I,————— (woman), take you,————— (man), to be my husband, according to the ordinances of God, to love and to cherish as long as we both shall live.

THE TOKEN

The minister shall take the bride's ring, hand it to the groom, instruct him to place it on the fourth finger of the bride's left hand and—while he holds the ring in place—repeat as follows:

With this ring I pledge my faith and trust. Receive it as a symbol of our endless union and our unbroken love.

If a groom's ring is used, the minister shall take it and hand it to the bride, instructing her in the same manner as he did the groom, and asking her to repeat as follows:

With this ring I pledge my faith and trust. Receive it as a symbol of our endless union and our unbroken love.

PRAYER

To the assembled guests, the minister shall say:
Let us pray.

Prayer shall then be offered with the couple kneeling before the minister.

PRONOUNCEMENT

After the bride and groom have risen from their

knees and are standing before the minister, he shall say:

Now that you, ————— (man), and ————— (woman), have consented together in holy matrimony, and pledged your faith to each other by giving and receiving of a ring (rings), before God and these witnesses—in the name of the Father, the Son, and the Holy Spirit, I pronounce you man and wife. What therefore God has joined let no man put asunder.

BENEDICTION

The following or some other suitable benediction may be used:

May this holy union ever be a perfect type of God's great love. May it be blessed and used that many souls shall find their places in the spotless Bride of Christ. Amen.

—Emil A. Balliet

WEDDING CEREMONY

INTRODUCTION

Addressing the assembled guests, the minister may say:

We are gathered today on this most happy occasion to join together this man and this woman in holy matrimony.

GIVING THE BRIDE

Following the introduction, the minister shall ask:

Who giveth this woman to be married to this man?

The father of the bride shall answer:

Her mother and I.

ADDRESS TO THE GUESTS

To the witnesses and guests, the minister may say:

Marriage is an institution of God. All our thinking on the subject has its basis in the divine revelation, the Holy Scriptures. God Himself was the originator of it when He said, "For this cause a man shall leave father and mother, and shall cleave to his wife and they twain shall be one flesh." It is apparent that our Maker instituted this as an experience of love, to provide his own idea of a proper social order and to provide that through well-ordered families truth and holiness might be transmitted from one age to another.

We learn from the Scriptures that Jesus honored a marriage festival with His presence, and I think that it is not without significance that He chose this

15

occasion to begin His miracles when He turned the water into wine. I think it is not out of order, either, that the Holy Spirit speaking through Paul selected the symbol of husband and wife as an apt emblem of the union that binds together Christ Himself and His own blood-bought, ransomed Church.

CHARGE

Speaking to the people who have come to be married, the minister shall say:

A relationship that is thus consecrated should not be formed thoughtlessly and irreverently, but advisedly and in the fear of God, knowing that He as the divine Author ordained and blessed matrimony. And now as in His sight and as you will answer in the day when all our hearts shall be made manifest, I charge you both that if there be any cause that should prevent your lawful union, you shall now speak.

If there be no impediment, the minister shall say to the man:

————— (man), wilt thou have this woman to thy wedded wife, to live together after God's ordinance in the holy estate of matrimony? Wilt thou love her, comfort her, honor her, and keep her in sickness and in health; and forsaking all others, keep thee only unto her as long as ye both shall live?

The man shall answer:

I will.

The minister shall then say to the woman:

16

————— (woman), wilt thou have this man to thy wedded husband, to live together after God's ordinance in the holy estate of matrimony? Wilt thou obey him and serve him, love, honor, and keep him in sickness and in health, and forsaking all others, keep thee only unto him as long as ye both shall live?

The woman shall answer:

I will.

Vows

The minister, taking the woman by the right hand and taking the man by the right hand, shall bring the hands together and instruct the couple to join hands.

Then the minister shall instruct the man to repeat after him:

I,————— (man), take thee,————— (woman), to my wedded wife, to have and to hold from this day forward, for better for worse, for richer for poorer, in sickness and in health, to love and to cherish till God by death doth separate us, and thereto I pledge my faith.

As the couple continue to join right hands, the minister shall instruct the woman to repeat after him:

I,————— (woman), take thee,————— (man), to my wedded husband, to have and to hold from this day forward, for better for worse, for richer for poorer, in sickness and in health, to love, to cherish, and to obey till God by death doth separate us, and thereto I pledge my faith.

TOKEN AND ADDRESS TO THE PARTIES

To the people who have come to be married, the minister shall say:

What token do you offer that you will faithfully fulfill these vows?

The ring shall be given to the minister, who shall hold it and say:

The circle—the emblem of eternity. Gold, the type of that which is least tarnished and most enduring, is to show how lasting and imperishable is the faith which is now mutually pledged.

As the union now formed is to be separated only by death, it becomes you both to consider the duties you solemnly assume. If these be remembered and faithfully discharged, they will add to the happiness of your life: lightening by dividing those inevitable sorrows, and heightening by doubling all its blessedness. However, if these obligations be neglected and violated, you cannot escape the keenest misery as well as the darkest guilt.

It is the responsibility of the husband to provide for the support of his wife—to shelter her from danger. It is his duty to cherish for her a manly and unalterable affection, it being the command of God's Word that husbands love their wives even as Christ loved the Church and gave His own life for her.

It is the duty of the wife to reverence and obey her husband and to put on the ornament of a meek and quiet spirit which in God's sight is an

18

ornament of great price, His Word commanding that wives be subject to their own husbands even as the Church is subject to Christ.

It is the privilege of both to delight in the company of the other, to remember that in interest and in affection they are to be henceforth undivided. It is their duty to preserve always the fidelity of this union.

The minister shall hand the ring to the man, instructing him to place it on the ring finger of the woman's left hand and repeat after him:

With this ring I thee wed, and with all my worldly goods I thee endow, in the name of the Father, and of the Son, and of the Holy Ghost.

If there is a groom's ring the minister shall take it in his hand and bless it. Then he shall hand it to the woman, instructing her to place it on the ring finger of the man's left hand and repeat after him:

With this ring I thee wed, in the name of the Father, and of the Son, and of the Holy Ghost.

PRONOUNCEMENT

To the assembled guests, the minister shall say:

Those whom God hath joined together let no man put asunder.

Forasmuch as————(man) and————(woman) have consented together in holy wedlock and witnessed the same before God and this company and thereto have given and pledged their faith each to the other, and have declared the same by giving and

19

receiving a ring and by joining hands: I pronounce that they are husband and wife, in the name of the Father, and of the Son, and of the Holy Ghost.

Prayer

This shall be an extemporaneous prayer for God's blessing on the marriage; and it may end with a benediction.

—*Fred Greve*

WEDDING CEREMONY

Address to the Guests

After the man and woman who are to be married have come to stand before the minister, he may speak to the assembled guests:

We are gathered in the sight of God and in the presence of this company to join together this man and this woman in holy matrimony.

The Bible teaches us that marriage is a holy institution, established in heaven by the divine wisdom and kindness of God, who said, "It is not good that man should be alone; I will make him an help meet for him." And who again said, "They two shall be one."

Jesus Christ the Son of God honored and sanctified the wedding in Cana of Galilee with His presence, and it was here that He wrought His first miracle, bringing cheer and joy to the host and his guests.

In thus beautifying this earthly union with the first recorded manifestation of His miracle-working power, He saw in it a symbol of the day to come when He Himself as the blessed Heavenly Bridegroom of the Church should lead "His own beloved," the mystical bride chosen and drawn by grace from among men, to that great "marriage supper of the Lamb" that God the Father Himself has ordained shall be celebrated when the victory of the Cross shall have been consummated.

In creation, Adam, the man, was first formed, then the woman, Eve, say the Scriptures, that the woman might be for the man, setting forth the humility, modesty, and gentleness that should characterize her kind.

Yet man, in being made last of all of God's creatures, was set forth as the best and most excellent of all of God's creative works.

So Eve's being made after Adam and out of him sets an honor upon the woman as being the glory of man.

If the man is the head, she is the crown—a crown to her husband. The man was dust refined, but the woman was doubly refined—one step further from the earth.

In being created from man, or out of man, she was not:

out of his head to dominate, or to be over him, nor

out of his feet to be under him, or trampled upon by him,

but

out of his side to be equal with him,

from under his arm to be protected by him, and near to his heart to be loved.

PRAYER

To the guests the minister shall say:

Let us pray:

Prayer should be for the full realization and appreciation of the meaning and blessings of marriage, and for a determination on the part of both the bride and groom to see these blessings worked out in their lives.

Renewal of Betrothal Pledge

To the man, the minister shall say:

————— (man), wilt thou have this woman to be thy wedded wife, to live together after God's holy ordinance, in the holy estate of matrimony? Wilt thou love her, comfort her, honor and keep her, in sickness and in health; and, forsaking all others, keep thee only unto her, so long as ye both shall live?

The man shall answer:

I will.

To the woman, the minister shall say:

————— (woman), wilt thou have this man to be thy wedded husband, to live together after God's holy ordinance, in the holy estate of matrimony? Wilt thou love him, honor and keep him, in sickness and in health; and forsaking all others, keep thee only unto him, so long as ye both shall live?

The woman shall answer:

I will.

Vows

————— (man), you may now take ————— (woman's) right hand in yours.

The man shall extend his right hand toward the woman with the palm turned up; the woman shall place her right hand in the man's hand with the palm turned down. The man shall cover her hand with his left hand.

The man shall then be instructed to repeat after the minister as follows:

I,————— (man), take thee,————— (woman), to be my wedded wife, to have and to hold from this day forward, for better for worse, for richer for poorer, in sickness and in health, to love and to cherish, till death do us part, according to God's holy ordinance, and thereto I plight thee my troth.

————— (woman), you may now take————— (man's) hand in your hand.

The woman shall extend her right hand toward the man with the palm turned up; the man shall place his right hand in the woman's hand with the palm turned down. The woman shall cover his hand with her left hand.

The woman shall then be instructed to repeat after the minister as follows:

I,————— (woman), take thee,————— (man), to be my wedded husband, to have and to hold from this day forward, for better for worse, for richer for poorer, in sickness and in health, to love and to cherish, till death do us part, according to God's holy ordinance, and thereto I plight thee my troth.

TOKEN

The minister shall ask for the ring; and, holding it in his hand, may say:

Let us meditate upon the symbolism of this golden circlet. Holy writ tells us that when God made a covenant with Noah, He set His bow in the cloud as a token of that covenant, and said, "I will look upon it that I may remember the everlasting covenant." From this we learn that it is well for us, when we enter into a solemn agreement to set aside some reminder.

You have selected this ring to be a token of your marriage covenant. It is made of gold which is a type of that which is least tarnished, and most enduring, fittingly representing the ties that bind husband and wife. The ring, an endless circle until broken by some outside force, is a symbol of the unbroken union which is to continue until broken by death.

The minister shall give the ring to the man, and instruct him to place it on the fourth finger of the bride's left hand and continue to hold it in place during the remainder of the ring ceremony. Aloud, the minister shall say:

Take this ring,————— (man), and place it upon the finger of————— (woman's) hand, and let it be the seal of your mutual fidelity and affection, and a memorial of this sacred service.

As the man continues to hold the ring in place, he shall repeat after the minister as follows:

With this ring I do thee wed, and with all my worldly goods I thee endow, in the name of the Father, and of the Son, and of the Holy Ghost. Amen.

CHARGE

Addressing both the bride and the groom, the minister shall continue:

Now let me speak to your hearts. I charge you both as you hope for happiness in your married life, to be true to these vows you have made to each

25

other. With your marriage, from this day, you begin life anew, with larger responsibilities.

————— (man), guard well this your bride who now commits herself into your keeping, and strive so to live in the Lord that no word or deed of yours shall cloud her brow with grief, or dim her eyes with tears.

————— (woman), it will be your part to strive to retain by your virtues the heart you have won by your graces.

And to you both, I would say: Let not your voices lose the tender tones of affection nor your eyes forget the tender ray with which they shone in courtship's day. And, greatest of all, let God be enthroned above all else at all times.

PRONOUNCEMENT

The couple shall be instructed to join right hands. Then the minister shall lay his hand upon the joined hands, and say:

And now, having heard you make these pledges of your affection, and take these vows of fidelity, I do, by the authority conferred upon me by the Church of Christ and by the laws of this commonwealth, pronounce you husband and wife, no longer twain, but now one, in the name of the Father, and of the Son, and of the Holy Spirit. Amen.

SALUTATION

The minister may now greet the couple for the first time as husband and wife.

Then the couple shall be instructed to turn so as to face the guests, and the minister shall say to the guests:

Allow me to present Mr. and Mrs.—————.

Following the presentation to the guests, the couple shall turn again to face the minister.

PRAYER

Then the minister shall say:

Let us pray.

The couple shall kneel before the minister who shall lay hands upon them and pray for God's blessing upon the life which they begin together.

DECLARATION

The man and woman shall arise from their knees and stand before the minister as he says:

Those whom God hath joined together, let no man put asunder.

BENEDICTION

One of the scriptural benedictions may be used, or a prayer of benediction.

—*T. Kermit Jeffrey*

27

WEDDING CEREMONY

ADDRESS

The parties standing before the minister, he shall say:

We are gathered together in the sight of God, and in the presence of this company to join together ————— (full name of groom) and————— (full name of bride) in holy matrimony, which is commended by St. Paul to be honorable among all men; and therefore is not to be entered into unadvisedly or lightly; but reverently, discreetly, soberly, and in the fear of God. Into this holy estate these two persons come now to be joined.

GIVING THE BRIDE

The minister shall then ask:

Who giveth this woman to be married to this man?

The person giving the bride away shall identify his relationship (father, brother, uncle, etc.) saying:

I, the————— (relationship). do.

VOWS

The couple shall be caused to join hands, and the minister shall ask the man to repeat after him:

I,————— (man's given name) , take thee,————— (woman's given name) , to be my wedded wife, for better for worse, for richer for poorer, in sickness and in health, to love and cherish, until death us do part, according to God's holy ordinance; and thereto I give thee my love.

In like manner the woman shall repeat:

I,————— (woman's given name), take thee,——
——— (man's given name), to be my wedded husband, to have and to hold, from this day forward, for better for worse, for richer for poorer, in sickness and in health, to love, honor, and cherish until death us do part, according to God's holy ordinance; and thereto I give thee my love.

THE TOKEN

If there is to be a giving of a ring, the minister shall ask:

What token do you give————— (given name of woman) of your love?

The ring shall be given to the minister as the groom answers:

A ring.

The minister shall give the ring to the groom, and say:

Please put it on her ring finger, and repeat after me these words: "With this ring I thee wed, and herewith I give thee my love and devotion so long as we both shall live."

If there is to be a giving of a second ring, the minister shall ask:

What token do you give————— (given name of man) of your love?

The groom's ring shall be given to the minister as the bride says:

A ring.

The minister shall give the ring to the bride, and say:

Please put it on his ring finger, and repeat after me these words: "With this ring I thee wed, and herewith I give thee my love and devotion so long as we both shall live."

PRONOUNCEMENT

The minister shall then address the audience, saying:

Forasmuch as———— (full name of man) and ———— (full name of woman) have consented together in holy wedlock, and have witnessed the same before God and this company, and hereto have given and pledged their love each to the other, and have declared the same by giving and receiving a ring, and by joining hands; I pronounce that they are husband and wife, in the name of the Father, and of the Son, and of the Holy Ghost. What God hath joined together never let man put asunder.

PRAYER

The minister shall say:

Let us pray.

Extemporaneous prayer shall be for God's blessing on the couple and for happiness and a life of Christian service for each of them.

—*James G. Mayo*

MARRIAGE SERVICE ADAPTED FROM THE BOOK OF COMMON PRAYER

ADDRESS

At the time appointed for solemnization of matrimony, the persons to be married shall stand before the minister, the man on the right hand and the woman on the left, and the minister shall say:

We are gathered here in the sight of God, and in the face of this company, to join together this man and this woman in holy matrimony; which is commended of St. Paul to be honorable among all men: and therefore is not by any to be entered into unadvisedly or lightly; but reverently, discreetly, advisedly, and in the fear of God. Into this holy estate, these two persons present come now to be joined. If any man can show just cause why they may not lawfully be joined together, let him now speak, or else hereafter forever hold his peace.

CHARGE

And, also, speaking unto the persons who are to be married, he shall say:

I require and charge you both, as ye will answer at the dreadful day of judgment, when the secrets of all hearts shall be disclosed, that if either of you know any impediment why ye may not be lawfully joined together in matrimony, ye do now confess it. For be ye well assured, that if any persons are joined together otherwise than as God's Word doth allow, their marriage is not lawful.

AFFIRMATION OF BETROTHAL PLEDGE

If no impediment shall be alleged, the minister shall say to the man:

Wilt thou have this woman to be thy wedded wife, to live together after God's ordinance, in the holy estate of matrimony? Wilt thou love her, comfort her, honor, and keep her, in sickness and in health; and, forsaking all others, keep thee only unto her, so long as ye both shall live?

The man shall answer:

I will.

Then shall the minister say to the woman:

Wilt thou have this man to be thy wedded husband, to live together after God's ordinance, in the holy estate of matrimony? Wilt thou obey him and serve him, love, honor, and keep him, in sickness and in health: and, forsaking all others, keep thee only unto him, so long as ye both shall live?

The woman shall answer:

I will.

GIVING THE BRIDE

Then shall the minister say:

Who giveth this woman to be married to this man?

VOWS

Then shall they give their troth to each other in this manner: the minister, receiving the woman at her father's or friend's hands, shall cause the man with his right hand to take the woman by her right hand, and to say after him as follows:

I,————— (man), take thee,————— (woman), to be my wedded wife, to have and to hold from this day forward, for better for worse, for richer for poorer, in sickness and in health, to love and to cherish, till death us do part, according to God's holy ordinance; and thereto I plight thee my troth.

Then shall they loose their hands; and the woman, with her right hand taking the man by his right hand, shall likewise say after the minister:

I,————— (woman), take thee,————— (man), to be my wedded husband, to have and to hold from this day forward, for better for worse, for richer for poorer, in sickness and in health, to love, cherish, and to obey, till death us do part, according to God's holy ordinance; and thereto I give thee my troth.

TOKEN

Then shall they again loose their hands; and the man shall give unto the woman a ring. And the minister taking the ring shall deliver it unto the man, to put it upon the fourth finger of the woman's left hand. And the man, holding the ring there, and taught by the minister, shall say:

With this ring I thee wed, and with all my worldly goods I thee endow: in the name of the Father, and of the Son, and of the Holy Ghost. Amen.

PRAYER

Then, the man leaving the ring upon the fourth finger of the woman's left hand, the minister shall say:

Let us pray.

O eternal God, Creator and Preserver of all mankind, Giver of all spiritual grace, the Author of everlasting life; send Thy blessing upon these Thy servants, this man and this woman; that, as Isaac and Rebekah lived faithfully together, so these persons may surely perform and keep the vow and covenant betwixt them made (whereof this ring given and received is a token and pledge), and may ever remain in perfect love and peace together, and live according to Thy laws; through Jesus Christ our Lord. Amen.

DECLARATION

Then shall the minister join their right hands together and say:

Those whom God hath joined together, let no man put asunder.

Then shall the minister speak unto the company:

Forasmuch as————— (man), and————— (woman) have consented together in holy wedlock, and have witnessed the same before God and this company, and thereto have given and pledged their troth, each to the other, and have declared the same by giving and receiving a ring, and by joining hands; I pronounce that they are man and wife, in the name of the Father, and of the Son, and of the Holy Ghost. Amen.

BLESSING AND BENEDICTION

And the minister shall add this blessing, the candidates kneeling, and the minister putting his hands upon their heads:

36

God the Father, God the Son, God the Holy Ghost, bless, preserve, and keep you: The Lord mercifully with His favor look upon you, and fill you with all spiritual benediction and grace; that ye may so live together in this life that in the world to come ye may have life everlasting. Amen.

A DOUBLE RING CEREMONY

To both the man and the woman the minister shall say:

We read in the Scriptures that when God made a covenant with Noah, He set a "bow" in the sky as a token thereof, and said, "I will look upon it that I may remember the everlasting covenant." From this we may learn that it is well for us, when we enter into a solemn agreement, to set apart some reminder of the promise which we have made.

Then addressing the man the minister shall say:

————— (man), what token do you give as evidence that you will keep your marriage vows?

The ring shall be given to the minister, and the minister shall say:

You have for this purpose selected a ring.

This ring is the token of your marriage covenant. It is made of precious and enduring metal, and thus fittingly represents the ties which bind husband and wife. The ring, an endless circle, until broken by some outside force, is a symbol of the unbroken "union" that should continue until broken by death.

Again addressing the man, the minister shall say:

————— (man), take this ring and place it upon the finger of your bride, and say after me:

I,————— (man), with this ring do wed thee, ————— (woman), and with my worldly goods I thee endow, and by this act declare in the presence of these witnesses that I take thee to be my beloved wife and that I will be unto thee a faithful husband.

To the woman the minister shall say:

————— (woman), what token do you give as evidence that you will keep your marriage vows?

The ring shall be given to the minister, and the minister shall say:

You, too, have selected a ring with its symbolism of enduring ties and unbroken union.

And, continuing to address the woman, the minister shall say:

————— (woman), take this ring and place it upon the finger of————— (man), and say after me:

I,————— (woman), with this ring do wed thee, ————— (man), and with my worldly goods I thee entrust, and by this act declare in the presence of these witnesses that I take thee to be my beloved husband and that I will be unto thee a faithful wife.

—*James B. McKeehan*

A DOUBLE RING CEREMONY

The minister shall take the ring from the groom's attendant and, as he says the following words, hand the ring to the groom.

Inasmuch now as the husband is the head of the wife, imparting to her his name and receiving her into his care and providence, I give you this ring that you may place it on the finger of this woman as a token that you receive her.

The man shall take the ring and place it on the woman's finger. Then the minister, addressing the man by name, shall say:

————— (man), just as this ring compasses———— —— (woman's) finger, so are you to compass her life with strength and protecting love.

The minister, addressing the woman by name, shall say:

————— (woman), you are to wear this ring as a token of the enclosing bond of reverence and faith which fulfills the perfect circle of duty which makes you one.

The minister takes the ring from the bride's attendant and, as he says the following words, hands the ring to the woman.

And now in turn, as you have agreed together in the providence of God and before these witnesses, I give you this ring that you may place it on the finger of this man as a token of your affection.

The woman shall take the ring and place it on

the man's finger. Then the minister, addressing the woman by name, shall say:

————— (woman), just as this ring compasses ————— (man's) finger, so are you to compass his life with encouragement and supporting love.

The minister, addressing the man by name, shall say:

————— (man), I charge you to wear this ring as a token of the enclosing bond of reverence and faith which fulfills the perfect circle of duty which makes you one.

—H. W. Thiemann

A CHARGE[1]

Forasmuch as all marriages which are contrary to God's Word are unlawful and void, I charge you before God and these witnesses that if any cause why you may not be joined in marriage does exist, you now confess it. If no such cause exists, you will now join your right hands.

[1] This charge might be used in place of the charge found in any of these marriage ceremonies.

GOLDEN WEDDING CEREMONY

ADDRESS

To the assembled guests, the minister may say:

We are gathered together here in the sight of God, and in the presence of this company to rejoice with this man and this woman on the occasion of their fiftieth wedding anniversary, and to join with them in the renewal of their marriage vows. They stand before us as an example of the blessedness of matrimony, which St. Paul commended as honorable among all men; and therefore not by any to be entered into unadvisedly, or lightly; but reverently, discreetly, advisedly, and in the fear of God. In this holy estate, these two have lived for fifty years— in a union which has ripened into a love and loyalty, and a devotion which has been an inspiration to all who have known them.

Now, in the presence of our Lord Jesus Christ who has led them through many experiences of both joy and difficulty, they give again to each other their hearts, their hands, and all that they have and are.

RENEWAL OF VOWS

Addressing the husband, the minister shall say:

————— (man), fifty years ago you pledged your loyalty to————— (woman) as your wedded wife, to live together after God's ordinance, in the holy estate of matrimony. You promised to love her, comfort her, honor, and keep her, in sickness and in health.

You further promised that, forsaking all others, you would keep yourself only unto her, so long as you both should live. During these fifty years you have been faithful to that pledge. Now again, at the beginning of the fifty-first year of your life together, in the presence of God, in the presence of your family, and in the presence of friends who have gathered for this happy occasion—will you renew these vows, pledging yourself to continue your devotion to her as long as you both shall live?

The man shall answer:

I will.

Addressing the wife, the minister shall say:

————— (woman), fifty years ago you pledged your loyalty to————— (man) as your wedded husband, to live together after God's ordinance, in the holy estate of matrimony. You promised to obey him and serve him, love, honor, and keep him, in sickness and in health. You further promised that, forsaking all others, you would keep yourself only unto him, so long as you both should live. During these fifty years you have been faithful to your pledge. Now—at the beginning of the fifty-first year of your life together, in the presence of God, in the presence of your family and in the presence of friends who have gathered for this happy occasion— will you renew these vows, pledging yourself to continue your devotion to him as long as you both shall live?

The woman shall answer:

I will.

TOKEN

Then shall the man give unto the woman a suitable token. And the minister, taking the token, shall deliver it unto the man to put it on the finger (or pin on the dress) of the woman. And the man, holding the woman by the hand, shall repeat after the minister:

With the giving of this token I renew my vow of love and loyalty. With sincere affection and with all my worldly goods I continue to thee endow. In the name of the Father, and of the Son, and of the Holy Ghost. Amen.

Then shall the woman give unto the man a suitable token. And the minister, taking the token, shall deliver it unto the woman to put on the finger (or pin on the person or otherwise wear) of the man. The woman, holding the man by the hand, shall repeat after the minister:

With the giving of this token I renew my vow of love and devotion. With sincere affection and with all my worldly goods I continue to thee endow. In the name of the Father, and of the Son, and of the Holy Ghost. Amen.

PRONOUNCEMENT

To the guests, the minister shall say:

Forasmuch as————— (husband's full name) and ————— (wife's full name) have consented together in the renewal of their marriage vows, and have witnessed the same before God and this company, and thereto have pledged their faith, each to the other, by giving and receiving a token, and by joining their hands, I now pray God's continued blessings and richest benediction upon them during the rest of their days as husband and wife together; in the name of the Father, and of the Son, and of the Holy Ghost. Amen.

PRAYER

The prayer may be by a close friend of the couple, or by one of the children picked by the family to be the family's representative.

—*William E. Pickthorn*

GOD'S PICTURE OF LOVE

There is one Love,
One Beauty, all divine,
And on earth what we know of beauty of love
Is but that reflected glory,
Mirrored here in flower, face, or soul,
That shines undimmed above.
How could we know—
We mortals of the clay—
What means the love of God to children of His care?
How could He help us understand?
He knew the way:
A story He would write us,
A picture He would draw,
And, as children looking at that picture fair,
We could know the glorious meaning;
We could read on earth the writing of God's hand.
And so today we meet to read again that story,
To gaze upon the beauty of that picture of God's love,
To hear Him say to us once more:
"As a bride awaits her bridegroom,
All arrayed in spotless splendor,
So the Church in holy gown awaits
His coming from above.
As the bridegroom loves his radiant bride,
So the Master loves His own."
And as we hear the promises to cherish and obey,
We can hear, like angel trumpets, resounding from
    His throne,

The promise that our Heavenly Groom
Will catch His bride away.
There is one Love,
One Beauty, all divine,
And these a simple mortal can never fully know.
And so God made a wedding,
To be the clearest view of love
That man will understand on earth below.
Thus the union of two mortals
Becomes a type immortal.
But flesh they were—each one alone;
Yet now, in marriage, they may be God's holy writ-
    ing—
A picture undistorted,
In which a true conception of the Love of God is
    shown.
So let us with joy and wonder feast our souls
As we share this holy type today,
And for these who paint for us anew God's finest
    picture
Let us pray:
Take them, oh God, and use them,
And make their love divine,
That through their yielded lives
Thy perfect Love may shine.

—*Mrs. Billie Davis*

Funerals

GENERAL USE

"When the Lord turned again the captivity of Zion, we were like them that dream. Then was our mouth filled with laughter, and our tongue with singing: then said they among the heathen, the Lord hath done great things for them. The Lord hath done great things for us; whereof we are glad. Turn again our captivity, O Lord, as the streams in the south. They that sow in tears shall reap in joy. He that goeth forth and weepeth, bearing precious seed, shall doubtless come again with rejoicing, bringing his sheaves with him."   (Ps. 126)

"Then answered Jesus and said unto them, Verily, verily, I say unto you, The Son can do nothing of himself, but what he seeth the Father do: for what things soever he doeth, these also doeth the Son likewise. For the Father loveth the Son, and sheweth him all things that himself doeth: and he will shew him greater works than these, that ye may marvel. For as the Father raiseth up the dead, and quickeneth them; even so the Son quickeneth whom he will. For the Father judgeth no man, but hath committed all judgment unto the Son: that all men should honour the Son, even as they honour the Father. He that honoureth not the Son honoureth not the Father which hath sent him. Verily, verily, I say unto you, He that heareth my word, and believeth

51

on him that sent me, hath everlasting life, and shall not come into condemnation; but is passed from death unto life. Verily, verily, I say unto you, The hour is coming, and now is, when the dead shall hear the voice of the Son of God: and they that hear shall live. For as the Father hath life in himself; so hath he given to the Son to have life in himself; and hath given him authority to execute judgment also, because he is the Son of man. Marvel not at this: for the hour is coming, in the which all that are in the graves shall hear his voice, and shall come forth; they that have done good, unto the resurrection of life; and they that have done evil, unto the resurrection of damnation." (John 5:19-29)

"Let not your heart be troubled: ye believe in God, believe also in me. In my Father's house are many mansions: if it were not so, I would have told you. I go to prepare a place for you. And if I go and prepare a place for you, I will come again, and receive you unto myself; that where I am, there ye may be also. And whither I go ye know, and the way ye know. Thomas saith unto him, Lord, we know not whither thou goest; and how can we know the way? Jesus saith unto him, I am the way, the truth, and the life: no man cometh unto the Father, but by me." (John 14:1-6)

"For as many as are led by the Spirit of God, they are the sons of God. For ye have not received the spirit of bondage again to fear; but ye have received the Spirit of adoption, whereby we cry,

Abba, Father. The Spirit itself beareth witness with our spirit, that we are the children of God: and if children, then heirs; heirs of God, and joint-heirs with Christ; if so be that we suffer with him, that we may be also glorified together. For I reckon that the sufferings of this present time are not worthy to be compared with the glory which shall be revealed in us. For the earnest expectation of the creature waiteth for the manifestation of the sons of God."

(Rom. 8:14-19)

"But now is Christ risen from the dead, and become the firstfruits of them that slept. For since by man came death, by man came also the resurrection of the dead. For as in Adam all die, even so in Christ shall all be made alive. But every man in his own order: Christ the firstfruits; afterward they that are Christ's at his coming. Then cometh the end, when he shall have delivered up the kingdom to God, even the Father; when he shall have put down all rule and all authority and power. For he must reign, till he hath put all enemies under his feet. The last enemy that shall be destroyed is death. For he hath put all things under his feet. But when he saith all things are put under him, it is manifest that he is excepted, which did put all things under him. And when all things shall be subdued unto him, then shall the Son also himself be subject unto him that put all things under him, that God may be all in all. Else what shall they do which are baptized for the dead, if the dead rise not at all? why are they then baptized for the dead? And why stand we in jeopardy every hour? I protest by your rejoicing which I have in Christ Jesus our Lord, I die daily. If after the manner of men I have fought with beasts at Ephesus, what advantageth it me, if the dead rise not? let us eat and drink; for to morrow we die. Be not deceived: evil communications corrupt good manners. Awake to righteousness, and sin not; for some have not the knowledge of God: I speak this to your shame. But some man will say, How are the dead raised up? and with what body do they come? Thou fool, that which thou sowest is not quickened, except it die: and that which thou sowest, thou sowest not that body that shall be, but bare grain, it may chance of wheat, or of some other grain: but God giveth it a body as it hath pleased him, and to every seed his own body. All flesh is not the same flesh: but there is one kind of flesh of men, another flesh of beasts, another of fishes, and another of birds. There are also celestial bodies, and bodies terrestrial: but the glory of the celestial is one, and the glory of the terrestrial is another. There is one glory of the sun, and another glory of the moon, and another glory of the stars: for one star differeth from another star in glory. So also is the resurrection of the dead. It is sown in corruption; it is raised in incorruption: it is sown in dishonour; it is raised in glory: it is sown in weakness; it is raised in power: it is sown a natural body; it is raised a spiritual body. There is a natural body, and there

is a spiritual body. And so it is written, The first
man Adam was made a living soul; the last Adam
was made a quickening spirit. Howbeit that was not
first which is spiritual, but that which is natural;
and afterward that which is spiritual. The first man
is of the earth, earthy: the second man is the Lord
from heaven. As is the earthy, such are they also
that are earthy: and as is the heavenly, such are
they also that are heavenly. And as we have borne
the image of the earthy, we shall also bear the
image of the heavenly. Now this I say, brethren, that
flesh and blood cannot inherit the kingdom of God;
neither doth corruption inherit incorruption. Behold, I shew you a mystery; We shall not all sleep,
but we shall all be changed, in a moment, in the
twinkling of an eye, at the last trump: for the
trumpet shall sound, and the dead shall be raised
incorruptible, and we shall be changed. For this
corruptible must put on incorruption, and this mortal
must put on immortality. So when this corruptible
shall have put on incorruption, and this mortal shall
have put on immortality, then shall be brought to
pass the saying that is written, Death is swallowed
up in victory. O death, where is thy sting? O grave,
where is thy victory? The sting of death is sin; and
the strength of sin is the law. But thanks be to
God, which giveth us the victory through our Lord
Jesus Christ. Therefore, my beloved brethren, be
ye stedfast, unmoveable, always abounding in the
work of the Lord, forasmuch as ye know that your
labour is not in vain in the Lord." (1 Cor. 15:20-58)

"We having the same spirit of faith, according as it is written, I believed, and therefore have I spoken; we also believe, and therefore speak; knowing that he which raised up the Lord Jesus shall raise up us also by Jesus, and shall present us with you. For all things are for your sakes, that the abundant grace might through the thanksgiving of many redound to the glory of God. For which cause we faint not; but though our outward man perish, yet the inward man is renewed day by day. For our light affliction, which is but for a moment, worketh for us a far more exceeding and eternal weight of glory; while we look not at the things which are seen, but at the things which are not seen: for the things which are seen are temporal; but the things which are not seen are eternal. For we know that if our earthly house of this tabernacle were dissolved, we have a building of God, an house not made with hands, eternal in the heavens. For in this we groan, earnestly desiring to be clothed upon with our house which is from heaven: if so be that being clothed we shall not be found naked. For we that are in this tabernacle do groan, being burdened: not for that we would be unclothed, but clothed upon, that mortality might be swallowed up of life. Now he that hath wrought us for the selfsame thing is God, who also hath given unto us the earnest of the Spirit. Therefore we are always confident, knowing that, whilst we are at home in the body, we are absent from the Lord: (for we walk by faith, not by sight:) we are confident, I say, and willing rather to be absent from the body, and to be present with the Lord. Wherefore we labour, that, whether present or absent, we may be accepted of him. For we must all appear before the judgment seat of Christ; that every one may receive the things done in his body, according to that he hath done, whether it be good or bad." (2 Cor. 4:13 to 5:10)

"After this I beheld, and, lo, a great multitude, which no man could number, of all nations, and kindreds, and people, and tongues, stood before the throne, and before the Lamb, clothed with white robes, and palms in their hands; and cried with a loud voice, saying, Salvation to our God which sitteth upon the throne, and unto the Lamb. And all the angels stood round about the throne, and about the elders and the four beasts, and fell before the throne on their faces, and worshipped God, saying, Amen: Blessing, and glory, and wisdom, and thanksgiving, and honour, and power, and might, be unto our God for ever and ever. Amen. And one of the elders answered, saying unto me, What are these which are arrayed in white robes? and whence came they? And I said unto him, Sir, thou knowest. And he said to me, These are they which came out of great tribulation, and have washed their robes, and made them white in the blood of the Lamb. Therefore are they before the throne of God, and serve him day and night in his temple: and he that sitteth on the throne shall dwell among them. They shall hunger no more, neither thirst any more; neither shall the sun light on them, nor any heat.

For the Lamb which is in the midst of the throne shall feed them, and shall lead them unto living fountains of waters: and God shall wipe away all tears from their eyes." (Rev. 7:9-17)

"And I saw a new heaven and a new earth: for the first heaven and the first earth were passed away; and there was no more sea. And I John saw the holy city, new Jerusalem, coming down from God out of heaven, prepared as a bride adorned for her husband. And I heard a great voice out of heaven saying, Behold, the tabernacle of God is with men, and he will dwell with them, and they shall be his people, and God himself shall be with them, and be their God. And God shall wipe away all tears from their eyes; and there shall be no more death, neither sorrow, nor crying, neither shall there be any more pain: for the former things are passed away. And he that sat upon the throne said, Behold, I make all things new. And he said unto me, Write: for these words are true and faithful. And he said unto me, It is done. I am Alpha and Omega, the beginning and the end. I will give unto him that is athirst of the fountain of the water of life freely. He that overcometh shall inherit all things; and I will be his God, and he shall be my son." (Rev. 21:1-7)

"And he shewed me a pure river of water of life, clear as crystal, proceeding out of the throne of God and of the Lamb. In the midst of the street of it, and on either side of the river, was there the tree of life, which bare twelve manner of fruits, and yielded her fruit every month: and the leaves of the tree were for the healing of the nations. And there shall be no more curse: but the throne of God and of the Lamb shall be in it; and his servants shall serve him: and they shall see his face; and his name shall be in their foreheads. And there shall be no night there; and they need no candle, neither light of the sun; for the Lord God giveth them light: and they shall reign for ever and ever. And he said unto me, These sayings are faithful and true: and the Lord God of the holy prophets sent his angel to shew unto his servants the things which must shortly be done. Behold, I come quickly: blessed is he that keepeth the sayings of the prophecy of this book." (Rev. 22:1-7)

A CHILD

"And it came to pass on the seventh day, that the child died. And the servants of David feared to tell him that the child was dead: for they said, Behold, while the child was yet alive, we spake unto him, and he would not hearken unto our voice: how will he then vex himself, if we tell him that the child is dead? But when David saw that his servants whispered, David perceived that the child was dead: therefore David said unto his servants, Is the child dead? And they said, He is dead. Then David arose from the earth, and washed, and anointed himself, and changed his apparel, and came into the house of the Lord, and worshipped:

then he came to his own house; and when he required, they set bread before him, and he did eat. Then said his servants unto him, What thing is this that thou hast done? thou didst fast and weep for the child, while it was alive; but when the child was dead, thou didst rise and eat bread. And he said, While the child was yet alive, I fasted and wept: for I said, Who can tell whether God will be gracious to me, that the child may live? But now he is dead, wherefore should I fast? can I bring him back again? I shall go to him, but he shall not return to me."   (2 Sam. 12:18-23)

"At the same time came the disciples unto Jesus, saying, Who is the greatest in the kingdom of heaven? And Jesus called a little child unto him, and set him in the midst of them, and said, Verily, I say unto you, Except ye be converted, and become as little children, ye shall not enter into the kingdom of heaven. Whosoever therefore shall humble himself as this little child, the same is greatest in the kingdom of heaven. And whoso shall receive one such little child in my name receiveth me."

(Matt. 18:1-5)

"Take heed that ye despise not one of these little ones; for I say unto you, That in heaven their angels do always behold the face of my Father which is in heaven. For the Son of man is come to save that which was lost. How think ye? if a man have an hundred sheep, and one of them be gone astray, doth he not leave the ninety and nine, and goeth into the mountains, and seeketh that which is gone astray? And if so be that he find it, verily I say unto you, he rejoiceth more of that sheep, than of the ninety and nine which went not astray. Even so it is not the will of your Father which is in heaven, that one of these little ones should perish."

(Matt. 18:10-14)

"And he took a child, and set him in the midst of them: and when he had taken him in his arms, he said unto them, Whosoever shall receive one of such children in my name, receiveth me: and whosoever shall receive me, receiveth not me, but him that sent me."   (Mark 9:36, 37)

"And they brought young children to him, that he should touch them: and his disciples rebuked those that brought them. But when Jesus saw it, he was much displeased, and said unto them, Suffer the little children to come unto me, and forbid them not: for of such is the kingdom of God. Verily I say unto you, Whosoever shall not receive the kingdom of God as a little child, he shall not enter therein. And he took them up in his arms, put his hands upon them, and blessed them."

(Mark 10:13-16)

A YOUNG MAN

"And it came to pass the day after, that he went into a city called Nain; and many of his disciples went with him, and much people. Now when he came nigh to the gate of the city, behold, there was a dead man carried out, the only son of his mother, and she was a widow: and much people of the city was with her. And when the Lord saw her, he had compassion on her, and said unto her, Weep not. And he came and touched the bier: and they that bare him stood still. And he said, Young man, I say unto thee, Arise. And he that was dead sat up, and began to speak. And he delivered him to his mother. And there came a fear on all: and they glorified God, saying, That a great prophet is risen up among us; and, That God hath visited his people. And this rumour of him went forth throughout all Judaea, and throughout all the region round about."

(Luke 7:11-17)

"Then said Thomas, which is called Didymus, unto his fellowdisciples, Let us also go, that we may die with him. Then when Jesus came, he found that he had lain in the grave four days already. Now Bethany was nigh unto Jerusalem, about fifteen furlongs off: and many of the Jews came to Martha and Mary, to comfort them concerning their brother. Then Martha, as soon as she heard that Jesus was coming, went and met him: but Mary sat still in the house. Then said Martha unto Jesus, Lord, if thou hadst been here, my brother had not died. But I know, that even now, whatsoever thou wilt ask of God, God will give it thee. Jesus saith unto her, Thy brother shall rise again. Martha saith unto him, ' know that he shall rise again in the resurrection at the last day. Jesus said unto her, I am the resurrection, and the life: he that believeth in me, though he were dead, yet shall he live: and whosoever liveth and believeth in me shall never die. Believest thou this? She saith unto him, Yea, Lord: I believe that thou art the Christ, the Son of God, which should come into the world. And when she had so said, she went her way, and called Mary her sister secretly, saying, The Master is come, and calleth for thee. As soon as she heard that, she arose quickly and came unto him. Now Jesus was not yet come into the town, but was in that place where Martha met him. The Jews then which were with her in the house, and comforted her, when they saw Mary, that she rose up hastily and went out, followed her, saying, She goeth unto the grave to weep there. Then when Mary was come where Jesus was, and saw him, she fell down at his feet, saying unto him, Lord, if thou hadst been here, my brother had not died. When Jesus therefore saw her weeping, and the Jews also weeping which came with her, he groaned in the spirit, and was troubled, and said, Where have ye laid him? They said unto him, Lord, come and see. Jesus wept. Then said the Jews, Behold how he loved him! And some of them said, Could not this man, which opened the eyes of the blind, have caused that even this man should not have died? Jesus therefore again groaning in himself cometh to the grave. It was a cave, and a stone lay upon it. Jesus said, Take ye away the stone. Martha, the sister of him that was dead, saith unto him, Lord, by this time he stinketh: for he hath been dead four days. Jesus saith unto her, Said I not unto thee, that, if thou wouldest believe, thou shouldest see the glory of God? Then they took away the stone from the place where the dead was laid. And Jesus lifted up his eyes, and said, Father, I thank thee that thou hast heard me. And I knew that thou hearest me always: but because of the people which stand by I said it, that they may believe that thou hast sent me. And when he thus had spoken, he cried with a loud voice, Lazarus, come forth. And he that was dead came forth, bound hand and foot with grave-clothes: and his face was bound about with a napkin. Jesus saith unto them, Loose him, and let him go. Then many of the Jews which came to Mary, and had seen the things which Jesus did, believed on him. But some of them went their ways to the Pharisees, and told them what things Jesus had done."

(John 11:16-46)

A YOUNG WOMAN

"While he spake these things unto them, behold, there came a certain ruler, and worshipped him, saying, My daughter is even now dead: but come and lay thy hand upon her, and she shall live. And Jesus arose, and followed him, and so did his disciples. And when Jesus came into the ruler's house, and saw the minstrels and the people making a noise, he said unto them, Give place: for the maid is not dead, but sleepeth. And they laughed him to scorn. But when the people were put forth, he went in, and took her by the hand, and the maid arose. And the fame hereof went abroad into all that land." (Matt. 9:18, 19, 23-26)

"And, behold, there cometh one of the rulers of the synagogue, Jairus by name; and when he saw him, he fell at his feet, and besought him greatly, saying, My little daughter lieth at the point of death: I pray thee, come and lay thy hands on her, that she may be healed; and she shall live. And Jesus went with him; and much people followed him, and thronged him. While he yet spake, there came from the ruler of the synagogue's house certain which said, Thy daughter is dead: why troublest thou the Master any further? As soon as Jesus heard the word that was spoken, he saith unto the ruler of the synagogue, Be not afraid, only believe. And he suffered no man to follow him, save Peter, and James, and John the brother of James. And he cometh to the house of the ruler of the synagogue,

65

and seeth the tumult, and them that wept and wailed greatly. And when he was come in, he saith unto them, Why make ye this ado, and weep? the damsel is not dead, but sleepeth. And they laughed him to scorn. But when he had put them all out, he taketh the father and the mother of the damsel, and them that were with him, and entereth in where the damsel was lying. And he took the damsel by the hand, and said unto her, Talitha cumi; which is, being interpreted, Damsel, I say unto thee, arise. And straightway the damsel arose, and walked; for she was of the age of twelve years. And they were astonished with a great astonishment."

(Mark 5:22-24; 35-42)

AN ELDERLY PERSON

"Behold, happy is the man whom God correcteth: therefore despise not thou the chastening of the Almighty: for he maketh sore, and bindeth up: he woundeth, and his hands make whole. He shall deliver thee in six troubles: yea, in seven there shall no evil touch thee. In famine he shall redeem thee from death: and in war from the power of the sword. Thou shalt be hid from the scourge of the tongue: neither shalt thou be afraid of destruction when it cometh. At destruction and famine thou shalt laugh: neither shalt thou be afraid of the beasts of the earth. For thou shalt be in league with the stones of the field: and the beasts of the field shall be at peace with thee. And thou shalt know that thy tabernacle shall be in peace; and thou shalt visit thy habitation, and shalt not sin. Thou shalt know also that thy seed shall be great, and thine offspring as the grass of the earth. Thou shalt come to thy grave in a full age, like as a shock of corn cometh in in his season."

(Job 5:17-26)

"Lord, make me to know mine end, and the measure of my days, what it is; that I may know how frail I am. Behold, thou hast made my days as an handbreadth; and mine age is as nothing before thee: verily every man at his best state is altogether vanity. Selah. Surely every man walketh in a vain shew: surely they are disquieted in vain: he heapeth up riches, and knoweth not who shall gather them. And now, Lord, what wait I for? my hope is in thee. Deliver me from all my transgressions: make me not the reproach of the foolish. I was dumb, I opened not my mouth; because thou didst it. Remove thy stroke away from me: I am consumed by the blow of thine hand. When thou with rebukes dost correct man for iniquity, thou makest his beauty to consume away like a moth: surely every man is vanity. Selah. Hear my prayer, O Lord, and give ear unto my cry; hold not thy peace at my tears: for I am a stranger with thee, and a sojourner, as all my fathers were. O spare me, that I may recover strength, before I go hence, and be no more."   (Ps. 39:4-13)

"Lord, thou hast been our dwelling place in all generations. Before the mountains were brought forth, or ever thou hadst formed the earth and the world, even from everlasting to everlasting, thou art God. Thou turnest man to destruction; and sayest, Return, ye children of men. For a thousand years in thy sight are but as yesterday when it is past, and as a watch in the night. Thou carriest them away as with a flood; they are as a sleep: in the morning they are like grass which groweth up. In the morning it flourisheth, and groweth up; in the evening it is cut down, and withereth. For we are consumed by thine anger, and by thy wrath are we troubled. Thou hast set our iniquities before thee, our secret sins in the light of thy countenance. For all our days are passed away in thy wrath: we spend our years as a tale that is told. The days of our years are threescore years and ten; and if by reason of strength they be fourscore years, yet is their strength labour and sorrow; for it is soon cut off, and we fly away."   (Ps. 90:1-10)

"Remember now thy Creator in the days of thy youth, while the evil days come not, nor the years draw nigh, when thou shalt say, I have no pleasure in them; while the sun, or the light, or the moon, or the stars, be not darkened, nor the clouds return after the rain: in the day when the keepers of the house shall tremble, and the strong men shall bow themselves, and the grinders cease because they are few, and those that look out of the windows be darkened, and the doors shall be shut in the streets, when the sound of the grinding is low, and he shall rise up at the voice of the bird, and all the daughters of musick shall be brought low; also when they shall be afraid of that which is high, and fears shall be in the way, and the almond tree shall flourish, and the grasshopper shall be a burden, and desire shall fail: because man goeth to his long home, and the mourners go about the streets: or ever the silver cord be loosed, or the golden bowl be broken, or the pitcher be broken at the fountain, or the wheel broken at the cistern. Then shall the dust return to the earth as it was: and the spirit shall return unto God who gave it." (Eccl. 12:1-7)

"For I am now ready to be offered, and the time of my departure is at hand. I have fought a good fight, I have finished my course, I have kept the faith: henceforth there is laid up for me a crown of righteousness, which the Lord, the righteous judge, shall give me at that day: and not to me only, but unto all them also that love his appearing." (2 Tim. 4:6-8)

A FAITHFUL CHRISTIAN

"Blessed is the man that walketh not in the counsel of the ungodly, nor standeth in the way of sinners, nor sitteth in the seat of the scornful. But his delight is in the law of the Lord; and in his law doth he meditate day and night. And he shall be like a tree planted by the rivers of water, that bringeth forth his fruit in his season; his leaf also shall not wither; and whatsoever he doeth shall prosper. The ungodly are not so: but are like the chaff which the wind driveth away. Therefore the ungodly shall not stand in the judgment, nor sinners in the congregation of the righteous. For the Lord knoweth the way of the righteous: but the way of the ungodly shall perish."

(Ps. 1)

"Bless the Lord, O my soul: and all that is within me, bless his holy name. Bless the Lord, O my soul, and forget not all his benefits: who forgiveth all thine iniquities; who healeth all thy diseases; who redeemeth thy life from destruction; who crowneth thee with lovingkindness and tender mercies; who satisfieth thy mouth with good things; so that thy youth is renewed like the eagle's. He hath not dealt with us after our sins; nor rewarded us according to our iniquities. For as the heaven is high above the earth, so great is his mercy toward them that fear him. As far as the east is from the west, so far hath he removed our transgressions from us. Like as a father pitieth his children, so the Lord pitieth them that fear him. For he knoweth our frame; he remembereth that we are dust. As for man, his days are as grass: as a flower of the field, so he flourisheth. For the wind passeth over it, and it is gone; and the place thereof shall know it no more. But the mercy of the Lord is from everlasting to everlasting upon them that fear him, and his righteousness unto children's children; to such as keep his covenant, and to those that remember his commandments to do them."   (Ps. 103:1-5, 10-18)

"Who can find a virtuous woman? for her price is far above rubies. The heart of her husband doth safely trust in her, so that he shall have no need of spoil. She will do him good and not evil all the days of her life. She stretcheth out her hand to the poor; yea, she reacheth forth her hands to the needy. Strength and honour are her clothing; and she shall rejoice in time to come. She openeth her mouth with wisdom; and in her tongue is the law of kindness. She looketh well to the ways of her household, and eateth not the bread of idleness. Her children arise up, and call her blessed; her husband also, and he praiseth her. Many daughters have done virtuously, but thou excellest them all. Favour is deceitful, and beauty is vain: but a woman that feareth the Lord, she shall be praised. Give her of the fruit of her hands; and let her own works praise her in the gates." (Prov. 31:10-12, 20, 25-31)

"Now faith is the substance of things hoped for, the evidence of things not seen. For by it the elders obtained a good report. Through faith we understand that the worlds were framed by the word of God, so that things which are seen were not made of things which do appear. By faith Abel offered unto God a more excellent sacrifice than Cain, by which he obtained witness that he was righteous, God testifying of his gifts: and by it he being dead yet speaketh. By faith Enoch was translated that he should not see death; and was not found, because God had translated him: for before his translation

71

he had this testimony, that he pleased God. But without faith it is impossible to please him: for he that cometh to God must believe that he is, and that he is a rewarder of them that diligently seek him. By faith Noah, being warned of God of things not seen as yet, moved with fear, prepared an ark to the saving of his house; by the which he condemned the world, and became heir of the righteousness which is by faith. By faith Abraham, when he was called to go out into a place which he should after receive for an inheritance, obeyed; and he went out, not knowing whither he went. By faith he sojourned in the land of promise, as in a strange country, dwelling in tabernacles with Isaac and Jacob, the heirs with him of the same promise: for he looked for a city which hath foundations, whose builder and maker is God." (Heb. 11:1-10)

SENTENCES FROM GOD'S WORD

"For I know that my redeemer liveth, and that he shall stand at the latter day upon the earth: and though after my skin worms destroy this body, yet in my flesh shall I see God: whom I shall see for myself, and mine eyes shall behold, and not another; though my reins be consumed within me."

(Job 19:25-27)

"He shall feed his flock like a shepherd: he shall gather the lambs with his arm, and carry them in his bosom, and shall gently lead those that are with young." (Isa. 40:11)

"For the Lord will not cast off for ever: but though he cause grief, yet will he have compassion according to the multitude of his mercies. For he doth not afflict willingly nor grieve the children of men." (Lam. 3:31-33)

"Blessed are they that mourn: for they shall be comforted." (Matt. 5:4)

"Jesus said unto her, I am the resurrection, and the life: he that believeth in me, though he were dead, yet shall he live: and whosoever liveth and believeth in me shall never die. Believest thou this?" (John 11:25, 26)

"Peace I leave with you, my peace I give unto you: not as the world giveth, give I unto you. Let not your heart be troubled, neither let it be afraid." (John 14:27)

"For I am persuaded, that neither death, nor life, nor angels, nor principalities, nor powers, nor things present, nor things to come, nor height, nor depth, nor any other creature, shall be able to separate us from the love of God, which is in Christ Jesus our Lord." (Rom. 8:38, 39)

"But as it is written, Eye hath not seen, nor ear heard, neither have entered into the heart of man, the things which God hath prepared for them that love him. But God hath revealed them unto us by his Spirit: for the Spirit searcheth all things, yea, the deep things of God." (1 Cor. 2:9, 10)

"Blessed be God, even the Father of our Lord Jesus Christ, the Father of mercies, and the God of all comfort; who comforteth us in all our tribulation, that we may be able to comfort them which are in any trouble, by the comfort wherewith we ourselves are comforted of God." (2 Cor. 1:3, 4)

"For our light affliction, which is but for a moment, worketh for us a far more exceeding and eternal weight of glory; while we look not at the things which are seen, but at the things which are not seen: for the things which are seen are temporal; but the things which are not seen are eternal." (2 Cor. 4:17, 18)

"For we know that if our earthly house of this tabernacle were dissolved, we have a building of God, an house not made with hands, eternal in the heavens." (2 Cor. 5:1)

"And I heard a voice from heaven saying unto me, Write, Blessed are the dead which die in the Lord from henceforth: Yea, saith the Spirit, that they may rest from their labours; and their works do follow them." (Rev. 14:13)

"And God shall wipe away all tears from their eyes; and there shall be no more death, neither sorrow, nor crying, neither shall there be any more pain: for the former things are passed away." (Rev. 21:4)

FUNERAL SERVICE

BRIEF—FOR A CHILD

BIBLE SENTENCE

"Comfort ye, comfort ye my people, saith your God. He shall feed his flock like a shepherd: he shall gather the lambs with his arm, and carry them in his bosom."   (Isa. 40:1, 11)

INVOCATION

The invocation should be brief and should simply ask for God to be present to help in this time of need. An appropriate form for the invocation on this occasion would be to ask the Shepherd Lord who tenderly cares for His lambs to hold the entire congregation in His arms that all might feel His comfort.

SCRIPTURE PORTION

"The Lord is my shepherd; I shall not want. He maketh me to lie down in green pastures: he leadeth me beside the still waters. He restoreth my soul: he leadeth me in the paths of righteousness for his name's sake. Yea, though I walk through the valley of the shadow of death, I will fear no evil: for thou art with me; thy rod and thy staff they comfort me. Thou preparest a table before me in the presence of mine enemies: thou anointest my head with oil; my cup runneth over. Surely goodness and mercy shall follow me all the days of my life: and I will dwell in the house of the Lord for ever."

(Ps. 23)

"And they brought young children to him, that he should touch them: and his disciples rebuked those that brought them. But when Jesus saw it, he was much displeased, and said unto them, Suffer the little children to come unto me, and forbid them not: for of such is the kingdom of God. And he took them up in his arms, put his hands upon them, and blessed them." (Mark 10:13, 14, 16)

PRAYER

This prayer may consist of thanksgiving to God for His care, and a request for God's comfort and sustaining grace to those who have been bereft of a loved one. It may include a request for God's blessing upon friends who have come to express their sympathy and love.

BENEDICTION

The following or any other suitable benediction may be used:

"Now the God of peace, that brought again from the dead our Lord Jesus, that great shepherd of the sheep, through the blood of the everlasting covenant, make you perfect in every good work to do his will, working in you that which is wellpleasing in his sight, through Jesus Christ; to whom be glory for ever and ever. Amen." (Heb. 13:20, 21)

—William E. Pickthorn

FUNERAL SERVICE

ORGAN PRELUDE

BIBLE SENTENCE

"Whether we live, we live unto the Lord; and whether we die, we die unto the Lord: whether we live therefore, or die, we are the Lord's. For to this end Christ both died, and rose, and revived, that he might be Lord both of the dead and living."

(Rom. 14:8, 9)

INVOCATION

This prayer might be addressed to God who, through His Son, died and rose again. It may request that He who is Lord both of the living and the dead give assurance of His presence.

SCRIPTURE PORTION

"Jesus said . . . I am the resurrection, and the life: he that believeth in me, though he were dead, yet shall he live: and whosoever liveth and believeth in me shall never die." (John 11:25, 26)

"God hath both raised up the Lord, and will also raise up us by his own power." (1 Cor. 6:14)

"God will redeem my soul from the power of the grave: for he shall receive me." (Ps. 49:15)

"For I know that my redeemer liveth, and that he shall stand at the latter day upon the earth: and . . . in my flesh I shall see God: whom I shall see for myself, and mine eyes shall behold, and not another."

(Job 19:25-27)

"The dead shall hear the voice of the Son of God: and they that hear shall live."   (John 5:25)

"God hath both raised up the Lord, and will also raise up us by his own power."   (1 Cor. 6:14)

"Like as Christ was raised up from the dead by the glory of the Father, even so we also should walk in newness of life."   (Rom. 6:4)

"For our conversation is in heaven; from whence also we look for the Saviour, the Lord Jesus Christ: who shall change our vile body, that it may be fashioned like unto his glorious body, according to the working whereby he is able even to subdue all things unto himself."   (Phil. 3:20, 21)

"Marvel not at this: for the hour is coming, in the which all that are in the graves shall hear his voice, and shall come forth."   (John 5:28, 29)

NOTE: *Favorite Bible passages of the deceased may be substituted for those of the above Bible reading.*

SONG

The following song may be sung as a solo or as a choral selection, or it may be read. A favorite song or poem of the deceased may be sung or read instead of the following selection.

Blessed assurance, Jesus is mine!
O what a foretaste of glory, divine!
Heir of salvation, purchased of God,
Born of His spirit, washed in His blood.

Chorus

This is my story, this is my song,
Praising my Saviour, all the day long;
This is my story, this is my song,
Praising my Saviour all the day long.

Perfect submission, perfect delight,
Visions of rapture now burst on my sight.
Angels descending, bring from above
Echoes of mercy, whispers of love.

Perfect submission, all is at rest,
I in my Saviour am happy and blest,
Watching and waiting, looking above,
Filled with His goodness, lost in His love.

REMARKS

*The remarks may center on the following ideas:
the favorite song just sung and its meaning to the
deceased, the ministries of the deceased in the com-
munity and church, the faith of the deceased and his
(her) hopes and desires for his (her) family and
friends.*

PRAYER

*Much of the concern of the prayer may be thanks-
giving for the life and ministry of the departed loved
one, and for the goodness of God who has taken His
child to be with Himself. God's comfort should be
asked for those who are bereaved.*

BENEDICTION

The following benediction or any other suitable one may be used:

"Now our Lord Jesus Christ himself, and God, even our Father, which hath loved us, and hath given us everlasting consolation and good hope through grace, comfort your hearts, and stablish you in every good word and work."　　　　(2 Thess. 2:16, 17)

ORGAN POSTLUDE

—William E. Pickthorn

FUNERAL SERVICE

BRIEF—FOR GENERAL USE

PRAYER

The opening prayer should be a request for God's presence and for God's blessing upon the service. It should also include a request for God's comfort for those who mourn. <u>Consolation</u>

SCRIPTURE PORTION

"God is our refuge and strength, a very present help in trouble. Therefore will not we fear, though the earth be removed, and though the mountains be carried into the midst of the sea; though the waters thereof roar and be troubled, though the mountains shake with the swelling thereof. Selah. There is a river, the streams whereof shall make glad the city of God, the holy place of the tabernacles of the Most High. God is in the midst of her; she shall not be moved: God shall help her, and that right early. The heathen raged, the kingdoms were moved: he uttered his voice, the earth melted. The Lord of hosts is with us; the God of Jacob is our refuge. Selah."   (Ps. 46:1-7)

"Lord, make me to know mine end, and the measure of my days, what it is; that I may know how frail I am. Behold, thou hast made my days as an handbreadth; and mine age is as nothing before thee: verily every man at his best state is altogether vanity. Selah. Surely every man walketh

81

in a vain shew: surely they are disquieted in vain: he heapeth up riches, and knoweth not who shall gather them. And now, Lord, what wait I for? my hope is in thee. Deliver me from all my transgressions: make me not the reproach of the foolish. I was dumb, I opened not my mouth; because thou didst it. Remove thy stroke away from me: I am consumed by the blow of thine hand. When thou with rebukes dost correct man for iniquity, thou makest his beauty to consume away like a moth: surely every man is vanity. Selah. Hear my prayer, O Lord, and give ear unto my cry; hold not thy peace at my tears: for I am a stranger with thee, and a sojourner, as all my fathers were. O spare me, that I may recover strength, before I go hence, and be no more." (Ps. 39:4-13)

SERMON

The message should be brief. It should be on the theme of comfort and hope, and it should include the plan of salvation.

BENEDICTION

A benediction is used only when the atmosphere of the service warrants it. If no benediction is to be used, the sermon may end with the word "Amen."

—Alvin I. Haun

FUNERAL SERVICE

ORGAN PRELUDE

SOLO

The following song, or any other appropriate hymn, may be sung as a solo or as a choral presentation; or it may be read as a poem.

Abide with me; fast falls the eventide;
The darkness deepens; Lord with me abide;
When other helpers fail, and comforts flee,
Help of the helpless, O abide with me.

Swift to its close ebbs out life's little day;
Earth's joys grow dim, its glories pass away;
Change and decay in all around I see;
O Thou, who changest not, abide with me.

I need Thy presence every passing hour;
What but Thy grace can foil the tempter's power?
Who like Thyself my guide and stay can be?
Through cloud and sunshine, O abide with me.

Hold Thou Thy cross before my closing eyes;
Shine through the gloom, and point me to the skies;
Heaven's morning breaks, and earth's vain shadows flee;
In life, in death, O Lord, abide with me.

SCRIPTURE PORTION

"The Lord is my light and my salvation; whom shall I fear? the Lord is the strength of my life; of

whom shall I be afraid? One thing have I desired
of the Lord, that will I seek after; that I may dwell
in the house of the Lord all the days of my life,
to behold the beauty of the Lord, and to enquire
in his temple. For in the time of trouble he shall
hide me in his pavilion: in the secret of his tabernacle shall he hide me; he shall set me up upon
a rock. And now shall mine head be lifted up above
mine enemies round about me: therefore will I offer
in his tabernacle sacrifices of joy; I will sing, yea,
I will sing praises unto the Lord. Hear, O Lord,
when I cry with my voice: have mercy also upon
me, and answer me. When thou saidst, Seek ye my
face; my heart said unto thee, Thy face, Lord, will
I seek. Wait on the Lord: be of good courage, and
he shall strengthen thine heart: wait, I say, on the
Lord."   (Ps. 27:1, 4-8, 14)

"For all things are for your sakes, that the abundant grace might through the thanksgiving of many
redound to the glory of God. For which cause we
faint not; but though our outward man perish, yet
the inward man is renewed day by day. For our
light affliction, which is but for a moment, worketh
for us a far more exceeding and eternal weight of
glory; while we look not at the things which are
seen, but at the things which are not seen: for the
things which are seen are temporal; but the things
which are not seen are eternal. For we know that
if our earthly house of this tabernacle were dissolved,

we have a building of God, an house not made with hands, eternal in the heavens."

(2 Cor. 4:15 to 5:1)

PRAYER

This prayer should be in the nature of a pastoral prayer, including thanksgiving to God for His goodness and a request for God's comforting presence with the bereaved. It may include thanksgiving for the expressions of sympathy from friends who have attended the service.

SOLO

This solo may be played as an organ solo, or it may be sung or read as a poem.

My faith looks up to Thee, Thou Lamb of Cal-
vary,
Saviour divine!
Now hear me while I pray, Take all my guilt away,
O let me from this day be wholly Thine.

When ends life's transient dream, When death's
cold, sullen stream
Shall o'er me roll;
Blest Saviour, then, in love, Fear and distrust
remove;
O bear me safe above, a ransomed soul!

SERMON

The Christian's hope of the resurrection is a suitable theme for the sermon. Suitable texts may be found in the Bible References at the beginning of this section of this book.

BENEDICTION

The following benediction from the Bible, or some other suitable benediction, should be used to close the service.

"The peace of God, which passeth all understanding, shall keep your hearts and minds through Christ Jesus. The grace of our Lord Jesus Christ be with you all. Amen."   (Phil. 4:7, 23)

—U. S. Grant

FUNERAL SERVICE

ORGAN PRELUDE

OBITUARY

The obituary usually begins with the full name, birth date, and date of death of the deceased. It usually contains a statement as to his (her) place of residence; and it may include a brief account of the person's life.

PRAYER

The prayer may begin with address to God, invoke His blessing on the service and contain requests for God's peace and sustaining grace to be made manifest to all who are present. There may be special requests for God's help for members of the family of the deceased.

SCRIPTURE PORTION

"Lord, thou hast been our dwelling place in all generations. Before the mountains were brought forth, or ever thou hadst formed the earth and the world, even from everlasting to everlasting, thou art God. Thou turnest man to destruction; and sayest, Return, ye children of men. For a thousand years in thy sight are but as yesterday when it is past, and as a watch in the night. So teach us to number our days, that we may apply our hearts unto wisdom. O satisfy us early with thy mercy; that we may rejoice and be glad all our days. Make us glad according to the days wherein thou hast afflicted us, and the years wherein we have seen evil. Let thy work appear unto thy servants, and thy glory unto their children. And let the beauty of the Lord our God be upon us: and establish thou the work of our hands upon us; yea, the work of our hands establish thou it."   (Ps. 90:1-4, 12, 14-17)

"For the Lord himself shall descend from heaven with a shout, with the voice of the archangel, and with the trump of God: and the dead in Christ shall rise first: then we which are alive and remain shall be caught up together with them in the clouds, to meet the Lord in the air: and so shall we ever be with the Lord. Wherefore comfort one another with these words."   (1 Thess. 4:16-18)

"After this I beheld, and, lo, a great multitude, which no man could number, of all nations, and kindreds, and people, and tongues, stood before the throne, and before the Lamb, clothed with white robes, and palms in their hands; and cried with a loud voice, saying, Salvation to our God which sitteth upon the throne, and unto the Lamb. And all the angels stood round about the throne, and about the elders and the four beasts, and fell before the throne on their faces, and worshipped God, saying, Amen: Blessing, and glory, and wisdom, and thanksgiving, and honour, and power, and might, be unto our God for ever and ever. Amen. And one of the elders answered, saying unto me, What are these which are arrayed in white robes? and whence came

they? And I said unto him, Sir, thou knowest. And
he said to me, These are they which came out of
great tribulation, and have washed their robes, and
made them white in the blood of the Lamb. Therefore are they before the throne of God, and serve
him day and night in his temple: and he that sitteth
on the throne shall dwell among them. They shall
hunger no more, neither thirst any more; neither
shall the sun light on them, nor any heat. For
the Lamb which is in the midst of the throne shall
feed them, and shall lead them unto living fountains
of waters: and God shall wipe away all tears from
their eyes."   (Rev. 7:9-17)

Music

*The music may be instrumental (such as organ),
or it may be a vocal solo or ensemble. The following
suggested hymn may be played, sung, or read as a
poem.*

O God, our help in ages past,
Our hope for years to come,
Our shelter from the stormy blast,
And our eternal home.

Under the shadow of Thy throne
Thy saints have dwelt secure;
Sufficient is Thine arm alone,
And our defense is sure.

A thousand ages in Thy sight
Are like an evening gone,
Short as the watch that ends the night
Before the rising sun.

O God, our help in ages past,
Our hope for years to come,
Be Thou our guard while troubles last,
And our eternal home.

REMARKS

*Remarks may include personal observations con-
cerning the deceased which would be of interest and
comfort to the bereaved. They may be based on the
minister's own personal observation of or relationship with the individual, or they may be based on
facts gleaned from conversations with the members
of the family.*

SERMON

*Suitable texts for sermons on resurrection and the
hope of eternal life may be found in the first part
of this section of this manual.*

MUSIC

*The following, or any suitable song or poem, may
be used:*

Saviour, like a shepherd lead us,
　　Much we need Thy tender care;
In Thy pleasant pastures feed us,
　　For our use Thy folds prepare:
Blessed Jesus, Blessed Jesus!
　　Thou hast bought us, Thine we are,
Blessed Jesus, Blessed Jesus!
　　Thou hast bought us, Thine we are.

Thou hast promised to receive us,
    Poor and sinful tho' we be;
Thou hast mercy to relieve us,
    Grace to cleanse, and power to free:
Blessed Jesus, Blessed Jesus!
    Early let us turn to Thee,
Blessed Jesus, Blessed Jesus!
    Early let us turn to Thee.

Early let us seek Thy favor,
    Early let us do Thy will;
Blessed Lord and only Saviour,
    With Thy love our bosom fill:
Blessed Jesus, Blessed Jesus!
    Thou hast loved us, love us still,
Blessed Jesus, Blessed Jesus!
    Thou hast loved us, love us still.

ORGAN POSTLUDE

—*James R. Swanson*

FUNERAL SERVICE

FOR GENERAL USE

PRAYER

This prayer should be an acknowledgment of the power, the love, and the presence of God.

SONG

Love Divine, so great and wondrous,
  Deep and mighty, pure, sublime;
Coming from the heart of Jesus,
  Just the same thro' tests of time.

Chorus

He the pearly gates will open,
  So that I may enter in;
For He purchased my redemption,
  And forgave me all my sin.

Like a dove when hunted, frightened,
  As a wounded fawn was I;
Broken-hearted, yet He healed me,
  He will heed the sinner's cry.

Love Divine, so great and wondrous,
  All my sins He then forgave;
I will sing His praise forever,
  For His blood, His pow'r to save.

In life's eventide, at twilight,
  At His door I'll knock and wait;
By the precious love of Jesus,
  I shall enter heaven's gate.

SCRIPTURE PORTION

"For I delivered unto you first of all that which I also received, how that Christ died for our sins according to the scriptures; and that he was buried, and that he rose again the third day according to the scriptures. Now if Christ be preached that he rose from the dead, how say some among you that there is no resurrection of the dead? But now is Christ risen from the dead, and become the first-fruits of them that slept. For since by man came death, by man came also the resurrection of the dead. For as in Adam all die, even so in Christ shall all be made alive. But every man in his own order: Christ the firstfruits; afterward they that are Christ's at his coming. But some man will say, How are the dead raised up? and with what body do they come? Thou fool, that which thou sowest is not quickened, except it die: and that which thou sowest, thou sowest not that body that shall be, but bare grain, it may chance of wheat, or of some other grain: but God giveth it a body as it hath pleased him, and to every seed his own body. All flesh is not the same flesh: but there is one kind of flesh of men, another flesh of beasts, another of fishes, and another of birds. There are also celestial bodies, and bodies terrestrial: but the glory of the celestial is one, and the glory of the terrestrial is another. There is one glory of the sun, and another glory of the moon, and another glory of the stars: for one star differeth from another star in glory. So also is the resurrection of the dead. It is sown in corruption; it is raised in incorruption: it is sown in dishonour; it is raised in glory: it is sown in weakness; it is raised in power: it is sown a natural body; it is raised a spiritual body. There is a natural body, and there is a spiritual body. And so it is written, The first man Adam was made a living soul; the last Adam was made a quickening spirit. Behold, I shew you a mystery; We shall not all sleep, but we shall all be changed, in a moment, in the twinkling of an eye, at the last trump: for the trumpet shall sound, and the dead shall be raised incorruptible, and we shall be changed. For this corruptible must put on incorruption, and this mortal must put on immortality. So when this corruptible shall have put on incorruption, and this mortal shall have put on immortality, then shall be brought to pass the saying that is written, Death is swallowed up in victory. O death, where is thy sting? O grave, where is thy victory? The sting of death is sin; and the strength of sin is the law. But thanks be to God, which giveth us the victory through our Lord Jesus Christ."

(1 Cor. 15:3, 4, 12, 20-23, 35-45, 51-57)

SERMON

The sermon should consist of a three-minute explanation as to why we do not sorrow as others. The message may end with the Bible passage on which the thought has been based.

BIBLE REFERENCE

"But I would not have you to be ignorant, brethren, concerning them which are asleep, that ye sorrow not, even as others which have no hope. For if we believe that Jesus died and rose again, even so them also which sleep in Jesus will God bring with him."   (1 Thess. 4:13, 14)

SONG

I will meet you in the morning,
    Just inside the Eastern Gate,
Then be ready, faithful pilgrim,
    Lest with you it be too late.

Chorus
I will meet you, I will meet you
    Just inside the Eastern Gate over there:
I will meet you, I will meet you,
    I will meet you in the morning over there.

Keep your lamps all trimmed and burning,
    For the Bridegroom watch and wait,
He'll be with us at the meeting,
    Just inside the Eastern Gate.

O the joys of that glad meeting
    With the saints who for us wait,
What a blessed, happy meeting,
    Just inside the Eastern Gate.

PRAYER

The focus of this prayer may be for the comfort of the bereaved and for spiritual blessings in the lives of the assembled friends.

BENEDICTION

"Now the God of hope fill you with all joy and peace in believing, that ye may abound in hope, through the power of the Holy Ghost."

(Rom. 15:13)

—*James Moore Evans*

FUNERAL SERVICE

OPENING PRAYER

A good pattern for prayer would include: acknowl-edgment of need for God, recognition of His power to meet all needs, recognition that He is waiting to bless, and an acknowledgment of His care even when men are not aware of His presence. It may contain the requests that: the sorrow be sanctified to the hearts of those present, that they shall be comforted, that the rod and staff of the Lord shall support them, that they may be made grateful for the eternal love of God and may enter into His peace. The prayer may include the requests that: those present go back to their daily lives eager to serve God, more inclined to love Him, supported by the Lord's strength and calmness and persuaded that nothing shall separate them from the love of God.

TRIBUTE TO THE DECEASED

The following, or some other Scripture portion may be used:

"Jesus said . . . I am the resurrection, and the life: he that believeth in me, though he were dead, yet shall he live: and whosoever liveth and believeth in me shall never die."   (John 11:25, 26)

"I know that my redeemer liveth, and that he shall stand at the latter day upon the earth: and though after my skin worms destroy this body, yet

99

in my flesh shall I see God: whom I shall see for myself, and mine eyes shall behold, and not another."

(Job 19:25-27)

After the reading from the Bible, the following or some other suitable tribute may be given:

These were the words of Job, and they express the faith of our departed friend and brother (sister), ————— (full name). It is fitting that you, who were his (her) friends in life should assemble here in the church he (she) loved so dearly and served so faithfully, to pay this last tribute to his (her) memory and to surround his (her) loved ones with our love and sympathy.

After this may follow remarks concerning the person's place and ministry in the church. There may also be remarks as to his faith and devotion to the Lord as shown in his personal and family life. The tribute may conclude in words similar to the following:

For you, his (her) friends and neighbors, and for his (her) beloved family, this is a time of sorrow and sadness as we realize that we will not walk beside him (her) here on earth again. That we will not again listen to his (her) footsteps or hear his (her) voice. But for our friend and loved one this is a time of rejoicing, a time of gladness. ————— (day of death) was his (her) Coronation Day. It was then that he (she) laid aside his (her) earthly body and entered into the presence of the Lord he (she) loved and served so faithfully.

This is not————— (name of deceased) we see before us. This is but the house in which he (she) lived for a time among us. He (she) is more alive than any person present in this sanctuary.

Song

A favorite hymn of the deceased shall have been chosen in advance for congregational singing. It may be announced as follows:

Let us at this time enter into his (her) joy as we sing together his (her) favorite hymn. It is hymn number—————, ————— (title of hymn) .

Scripture Portion

The Bible lesson may be taken from favorite passages of the deceased, or the following passages may be used, and may be introduced as follows:

And now we turn to the sacred Scripture verses in which he (she) found strength:

"The Lord is my shepherd; I shall not want. He maketh me to lie down in green pastures: he leadeth me beside the still waters. He restoreth my soul: he leadeth me in the paths of righteousness for his name's sake. Yea, though I walk through the valley of the shadow of death, I will fear no evil: for thou art with me; thy rod and thy staff they comfort me. Thou preparest a table before me in the presence of mine enemies: thou anointest my head with oil; my cup runneth over. Surely goodness and mercy shall follow me all the days of my life: and I will dwell in the house of the Lord for ever."   (Ps. 23)

"God is our refuge and strength, a very present help in trouble. Therefore will not we fear, though the earth be removed, and though the mountains be carried into the midst of the sea; though the waters thereof roar and be troubled, though the mountains shake with the swelling thereof."

(Ps. 46:1-3)

"Hast thou not known? hast thou not heard, that the everlasting God, the Lord, the Creator of the ends of the earth, fainteth not, neither is weary? there is no searching of his understanding. He giveth power to the faint; and to them that have no might he increaseth strength. Even the youths shall faint and be weary, and the young men shall utterly fall: but they that wait upon the Lord shall renew their strength; they shall mount up with wings as eagles; they shall run, and not be weary; and they shall walk, and not faint." (Isa. 40:28-31)

"For as many as are led by the Spirit of God, they are the sons of God. For ye have not received the spirit of bondage again to fear; but ye have received the Spirit of adoption, whereby we cry, Abba, Father. The Spirit itself beareth witness with our spirit, that we are the children of God: and if children, then heirs; heirs of God, and joint-heirs with Christ; if so be that we suffer with him, that we may be also glorified together. For I reckon that the sufferings of this present time are not worthy to be compared with the glory which shall be revealed in us. For the earnest expectation of the

creature waiteth for the manifestation of the sons of God. And we know that all things work together for good to them that love God, to them who are the called according to his purpose. What shall we then say to these things? If God be for us, who can be against us? He that spared not his own Son, but delivered him up for us all, how shall he not with him also freely give us all things? Who shall lay any thing to the charge of God's elect? It is God that justifieth. Who is he that condemneth? It is Christ that died, yea rather, that is risen again, who is even at the right hand of God, who also maketh intercession for us. Who shall separate us from the love of Christ? shall tribulation, or distress, or persecution, or famine, or nakedness, or peril, or sword? Nay, in all these things we are more than conquerors through him that loved us. For I am persuaded, that neither death, nor life, nor angels, nor principalities, nor powers, nor things present, nor things to come, nor height, nor depth, nor any other creature, shall be able to separate us from the love of God, which is in Christ Jesus our Lord."
(Rom. 8:14-19, 28, 31-35, 37-39)

"But I would not have you to be ignorant, brethren, concerning them which are asleep, that ye sorrow not, even as others which have no hope. For if we believe that Jesus died and rose again, even so them also which sleep in Jesus will God bring with him. For this we say unto you by the word of the Lord, that we which are alive and remain

103

unto the coming of the Lord shall not prevent them which are asleep. For the Lord himself shall descend from heaven with a shout, with the voice of the archangel, and with the trump of God: and the dead in Christ shall rise first: then we which are alive and remain shall be caught up together with them in the clouds, to meet the Lord in the air: and so shall we ever be with the Lord. Wherefore comfort one another with these words."

(1 Thess. 4:13-18)

SONG

A second favorite hymn of the deceased shall be sung as a congregational song, and may be announced as follows:

We will now sing another of————— (name of deceased) favorite hymns. It is hymn number—————, ————— (title).

PRAYER

A member of the executive board of the church shall have been selected in advance to represent the congregation in prayer. He may be presented as follows:

Mr.————— (name of board member), representing our————— (name of board), will lead us in prayer.

COMFORT FROM GOD'S WORD

Jesus said:

"Let not your heart be troubled: ye believe in God, believe also in me. In my Father's house are many mansions: if it were not so, I would have told you. I go to prepare a place for you. And if I go and prepare a place for you, I will come again, and receive you unto myself; that where I am, there ye may be also. And whither I go ye know, and the way ye know. Thomas saith unto him, Lord, we know not whither thou goest; and how can we know the way? Jesus saith unto him, I am the way, the truth, and the life: no man cometh unto the Father, but by me."   (John 14:1-6)

BENEDICTION

The benediction may be introduced in the following words:

The Lord be with you. Let us pray.

"The Lord bless thee, and keep thee: the Lord make his face shine upon thee, and be gracious unto thee: the Lord lift up his countenance upon thee, and give thee peace."   (Num. 6:24-26)

—*Norman E. Edwards*

FUNERAL SERVICE

ORGAN PRELUDE

SOLO

The following song may be sung as a solo or quartet. It may, if the place of meeting is suitable, be presented by a vocal ensemble.

In shady, green pastures, so rich and so sweet,
    God leads His dear children along;
Where the water's cool flow bathes the weary
    one's feet
    God leads His dear children along.

Chorus

Some thro' the waters, some thro' the flood,
Some thro' the fire, but all thro' the blood;
Some thro' great sorrow, but God gives a song,
In the night season and all the day long.

Sometimes on the mount where the sun shines so
    bright,
    God leads His dear children along;
Sometimes in the valley in the darkest of night,
    God leads His dear children along.

Tho' sorrows befall us, and Satan oppose,
God leads His dear children along;
Through grace we can conquer, defeat all our foes,
    God leads His dear children along.

107

Away from the mire, and away from the clay,
  God leads His dear children along;
Away up in glory, eternity's day,
  God leads His dear children along.

OBITUARY

SCRIPTURE PORTION

"The spirit of man is the candle of the Lord."
(Prov. 20:27)

"A man's gift maketh room for him, and bringeth him before great men." (Prov. 18:16)

"He that followeth after righteousness and mercy findeth life, righteousness, and honour."
(Prov. 21:21)

"A good name is rather to be chosen than great riches, and loving favour rather than silver and gold." (Prov. 22:1)

"By humility and the fear of the Lord are riches, and honour, and life." (Prov. 22:4)

"The heart of the prudent getteth knowledge; and the ear of the wise seeketh knowledge."
(Prov. 18:15)

"The eyes of the Lord preserve knowledge, and he overthroweth the words of the transgressor."
(Prov. 22:12)

"A man's heart deviseth his way: but the Lord directeth his steps." (Prov. 16:9)

"He that loveth pureness of heart, for the grace of his lips the king shall be his friend."
(Prov. 22:11)

"He that getteth wisdom loveth his own soul: he that keepeth understanding shall find good."
(Prov. 19:8)

"Wisdom is the principal thing; therefore get wisdom: and with all thy getting get understanding."
(Prov. 4:7)

"For wisdom is better than rubies; and all the things that may be desired are not to be compared to it."
(Prov. 8:11)

"The just man walketh in his integrity: his children are blessed after him."
(Prov. 20:7)

"To do justice and judgment is more acceptable to the Lord than sacrifice."
(Prov. 21:3)

"He that keepeth the commandment keepeth his own soul; but he that despiseth his ways shall die."
(Prov. 19:16)

"To do justice and judgment is more acceptable to the Lord than sacrifice."
(Prov. 21:3)

"The path of the just is as the shining light, that shineth more and more unto the perfect day."
(Prov. 4:18)

"He that dwelleth in the secret place of the most High shall abide under the shadow of the Almighty. I will say of the Lord, He is my refuge and my fortress: my God; in him will I trust. For he shall give his angels charge over thee, to keep thee in all thy ways. They shall bear thee up in their hands, lest thou dash thy foot against a stone."
(Ps. 91:1, 2, 11, 12)

"Strengthen ye the weak hands, and confirm

the feeble knees. Say to them that are of a fearful heart, Be strong, fear not: behold, your God will come with vengeance, even God with a recompence; he will come and save you. Then the eyes of the blind shall be opened, and the ears of the deaf shall be unstopped. Then shall the lame man leap as an hart, and the tongue of the dumb sing: for in the wilderness shall waters break out, and streams in the desert. And the parched ground shall become a pool, and the thirsty land springs of water: in the habitation of dragons, where each lay, shall be grass with reeds and rushes. And an highway shall be there, and a way, and it shall be called The way of holiness; the unclean shall not pass over it; but it shall be for those: the wayfaring men, though fools, shall not err therein. No lion shall be there, nor any ravenous beast shall go up thereon, it shall not be found there; but the redeemed shall walk there: and the ransomed of the Lord shall return, and come to Zion with songs and everlasting joy upon their heads: they shall obtain joy and gladness, and sorrow and sighing shall flee away." (Isa. 35:3-10)

"For our conversation is in heaven: from whence also we look for the Saviour, the Lord Jesus Christ: who shall change our vile body, that it may be fashioned like unto his glorious body, according to the working whereby he is able even to subdue all things unto himself." (Phil. 3:20, 21)

"For we know that if our earthly house of this tabernacle were dissolved, we have a building of God, an house not made with hands, eternal in the heavens. For in this we groan, earnestly desiring to be clothed upon with our house which is from heaven: if so be that being clothed we shall not be found naked. For we that are in this tabernacle do groan, being burdened: not for that we would be unclothed, but clothed upon, that mortality might be swallowed up of life. Now he that hath wrought us for the selfsame thing is God, who also hath given unto us the earnest of the Spirit. Therefore we are always confident, knowing that, whilst we are at home in the body, we are absent from the Lord: (for we walk by faith, not by sight:) we are confident, I say, and willing rather to be absent from the body, and to be present with the Lord. Wherefore we labour, that, whether present or absent, we may be accepted of him." (2 Cor. 5:1-9)

PRAYER

A leader in the church or a denominational official may be asked in advance to pray. A civic leader who is known to be a Christian may also be called on to lead in prayer.

ADDRESS

The first speaker may use as his theme the certainty of the resurrection of believers, and the coming of Christ as the blessed hope of the church.

SOLO

So precious is Jesus, my Saviour, my King,
His praise all the day long with rapture I sing;
To Him in my weakness for strength I can cling,
   For He is so precious to me.

Chorus

For He is so precious to me,
For He is so precious to me;
'Tis heaven below My Redeemer to know,
    For He is so precious to me.

He stood at my heart's door 'mid sunshine and rain,
And patiently waited an entrance to gain;
What shame that so long He entreated in vain,
    For He is so precious to me.

I stand on the mountain of blessing at last,
No cloud in the heavens a shadow to cast;
His smile is upon me, the valley is past,
    For He is so precious to me.

I praise Him because He appointed a place,
Where, some day, thro' faith in His wonderful grace;
I know I shall see Him—shall look on His face,
    For He is so precious to me.

Address

The second speaker may use as his theme the privilege of, God's call to, and the responsibilities and rewards of a life of service to God and to others.

Tribute

One or more of the people who were closely associated with the deceased in life may be asked in advance to prepare brief statements of appreciation.

TELEGRAMS

A person shall be appointed in advance to prepare and read excerpts from telegrams, letters, and other messages of condolence.

MUSIC

A hymn may be played or sung, or may be read as a poem. The following old hymn is effective as a quartet.

Amazing grace! how sweet the sound,
    That saved a wretch like me!
I once was lost, but now am found,
    Was blind, but now I see;

'Twas grace that taught my heart to fear,
    And grace my fears relieved;
How precious did that grace appear
    The hour I first believed!

Thro' many dangers, toils, and snares,
    I have already come;
'Tis grace hath bro't me safe thus far,
    And grace will lead me home.

When we've been there ten thousand years,
    Bright shining as the sun,
We've no less days to sing God's praise
    Than when we first begun.

BENEDICTION

"Now unto the King eternal, immortal, invisible, the only wise God, be honour and glory for ever and ever. Amen." (1 Tim. 1:17)

ORGAN POSTLUDE

—Raymond P. Murray

Burial Services

BIBLE REFERENCES

"In the sweat of thy face shalt thou eat bread, till thou return unto the ground; for out of it wast thou taken: for dust thou art, and unto dust shalt thou return." (Gen. 3:19)

"For I know that my redeemer liveth, and that he shall stand at the latter day upon the earth: and though after my skin worms destroy this body, yet in my flesh shall I see God: whom I shall see for myself, and mine eyes shall behold, and not another; though my reins be consumed within me." (Job 19:25-27)

"All flesh shall perish together, and man shall turn again unto dust." (Job 34:15)

"Thou hidest thy face, they are troubled: thou takest away their breath, they die, and return to their dust." (Ps. 104:29)

"All go unto one place; all are of the dust, and all turn to dust again." (Eccl. 3:20)

"Then shall the dust return to the earth as it was: and the spirit shall return unto God who gave it." (Eccl. 12:7)

"Jesus said unto her, I am the resurrection, and the life: he that believeth in me, though he were dead, yet shall he live." (John 11:25)

—Selected by *Wallace Bragg*

BURIAL SERVICE

COMFORT FROM GOD'S WORD

"For our light affliction, which is but for a moment, worketh for us a far more exceeding and eternal weight of glory; while we look not at the things which are seen, but at the things which are not seen: for the things which are seen are temporal; but the things which are not seen are eternal."

(2 Cor. 4:17, 18)

COMMITTAL STATEMENT

Forasmuch as it has pleased Almighty God of His mercy to take back to Himself the soul of our beloved ————— (name), we therefore commit his (her) body to the ground; earth to earth, ashes to ashes, dust to dust; in the sure and certain hope that the spirit which has returned unto God who gave it will be reunited with his (her) resurrected body at the second coming of Christ, when "the Lord himself shall descend from heaven with a shout, with the voice of the archangel, and with the trump of God." "For the trumpet shall sound, and the dead shall be raised incorruptible." "For this corruptible must put on incorruption and this mortal must put on immortality." "Then shall be brought to pass the saying that is written, Death is swallowed up in victory."

PRAYER

BENEDICTION

"The grace of the Lord Jesus Christ, and the love of God, and the communion of the Holy Ghost, be with you all. Amen." (2 Cor. 13:14)

—William E. Pickthorn

BURIAL SERVICE

COMFORT FROM GOD'S WORD

"Behold, I shew you a mystery; We shall not all sleep, but we shall all be changed, in a moment, in the twinkling of an eye, at the last trump: for the trumpet shall sound, and the dead shall be raised incorruptible, and we shall be changed. For this corruptible must put on incorruption, and this mortal must put on immortality. So when this corruptible shall have put on incorruption, and this mortal shall have put on immortality, then shall be brought to pass the saying that is written, Death is swallowed up in victory. O death, where is thy sting? O grave, where is thy victory? The sting of death is sin; and the strength of sin is the law. But thanks be to God, which giveth us the victory through our Lord Jesus Christ. Therefore, my beloved brethren, be ye stedfast, unmoveable, always abounding in the work of the Lord, forasmuch as ye know that your labour is not in vain in the Lord."

(1 Cor. 15:51-58)

COMMITTAL STATEMENT

"The Lord is my shepherd; I shall not want. He maketh me to lie down in green pastures: he leadeth me beside the still waters. He restoreth my soul: he leadeth me in the paths of righteousness for his name's sake. Yea, though I walk through the valley of the shadow of death, I will fear no evil: for

118

thou art with me; thy rod and thy staff they comfort me. Thou preparest a table before me in the presence of mine enemies: thou anointest my head with oil; my cup runneth over."

Surely goodness and mercy have followed me all the days of my life and I,————— (name of the deceased), will dwell in the house of the Lord for ever.

(After the Twenty-third Psalm).

PRAYER

This prayer should be a brief petition for the comfort of the family.

BENEDICTION

"Grace, mercy, and peace, from God the Father and Christ Jesus our Lord."　　　(2 Tim. 1:2)

PERSONAL WORD OF COMFORT

After the benediction a personal word of concern and comfort should be spoken to each member of the family of the deceased. A suitable expression is:
God bless you and comfort you.

—T. Kermit Jeffrey

BURIAL SERVICE

COMMITTAL STATEMENT

Inasmuch as Almighty God—with whom do live the spirits of them that depart hence in the Lord, and with whom the souls of the faithful, after they are delivered from the burden of the flesh, are in joy and peace with Him—inasmuch as He has taken unto Himself the soul of our departed brother (sister), we commit the earthly house of his habitation back to the ground from which it came; earth to earth, ashes to ashes, dust to dust; in the assurance that "if the earthly house of our tabernacle be dissolved, we have a building of God, an house not made with hands, eternal in the heavens."

PRAYER

—James R. Swanson

BURIAL SERVICE

COMFORT FROM GOD'S WORD

"I would not have you to be ignorant, brethren, concerning them which are asleep, that ye sorrow not, even as others which have no hope. For if we believe that Jesus died and rose again, even so them also which sleep in Jesus will God bring with him. For this we say unto you by the word of the Lord, that we which are alive and remain unto the coming of the Lord shall not prevent them which are asleep. For the Lord himself shall descend from heaven with a shout, with the voice of the archangel, and with the trump of God: and the dead in Christ shall rise first: then we which are alive and remain shall be caught up together with them in the clouds, to meet the Lord in the air: and so shall we ever be with the Lord. Wherefore comfort one another with these words." (1 Thess. 4:13-18)

PRAYER

The prayer should be a petition for the comfort of God to be given to all present; for God's blessing on any dedication of lives which people may make to Him; for God's guidance to lead each of those present into His best for their future in this life and in eternity.

BENEDICTION

"Grace be with you, mercy, and peace, from God

the Father, and from the Lord Jesus Christ, the
Son of the Father, in truth and love." (2 John 3)

—U. S. Grant

BURIAL SERVICE

Comfort from God's Word

"Let not your heart be troubled: ye believe in God, believe also in me. In my Father's house are many mansions: if it were not so, I would have told you. I go to prepare a place for you. And if I go and prepare a place for you, I will come again, and receive you unto myself; that where I am, there ye may be also. And whither I go ye know, and the way ye know. Thomas saith unto him, Lord, we know not whither thou goest; and how can we know the way? Jesus saith unto him, I am the way, the truth, and the life: no man cometh unto the Father, but by me." (John 14:1-6)

Address

The address may be in the nature of a brief sermon, or it may consist of affirmations of faith and comments of appreciation of the life and ministry of the deceased.

Committal Statement

————— (name) is not here. He (she) stands in the presence of the Lord who said to one dying on a cross, "Today shalt thou be with me in paradise." What lies before us is but the earthly tabernacle, the house in which he (she) lived among us for a time. Tenderly and reverently we commit that house to the grave. The body returns to the earth from which it came; earth to earth, ashes to ashes, dust to dust. The spirit returns to God who gave it, waiting the day when both spirit and body shall again be united at the coming of the Lord; "for the Lord himself shall descend from heaven with a shout, with the voice of the archangel, and with the trump of God: and the dead in Christ shall rise." "For this corruptible must put on incorruption, and this mortal must put on immortality." "Then shall be brought to pass the saying that is written, Death is swallowed up in victory."

COMMITTAL PRAYER

This prayer should commend into the hands of the Lord those who remain in this life that God may work in them those things which are well-pleasing in His sight. The hearers may also be committed to the comfort of God and to the peace which He alone can give.

THE LORD'S PRAYER

"Our Father which art in heaven, Hallowed be thy name. Thy kingdom come. Thy will be done in earth, as it is in heaven. Give us this day our daily bread. And forgive us our debts, as we forgive our debtors. And lead us not into temptation, but deliver us from evil: for thine is the kingdom, and the power, and the glory, for ever. Amen."

(Matt. 6:9-13)

BENEDICTION

"Grace be unto you, and peace, from God our Father, and from the Lord Jesus Christ."

(1 Cor. 1:3)

—*William E. Pickthorn*

BURIAL SERVICE

COMFORT FROM GOD'S WORD

"Well done, good and faithful servant; thou hast been faithful over a few things, I will make thee ruler over many things: enter thou into the joy of thy lord." (Matt. 25:23)

POEM[1]

Servant of God, well done!
Rest from thy loved employ:
The battle fought, the victory won,
Enter thy Master's joy.

The pains of death are past,
Labour and sorrow cease
And life's long warfare closed at last,
Thy soul is found in peace.

SONG [2]

If I asked for things that I should not ask for
If I prayed for things selfishly
If I asked for myself and not for my neighbor
Lift this veil from my eyes, let me see:

"Not my will, Thine be done," prayed Jesus;
May the same prayer be mine every day;
When this robe of flesh that I wear
Makes me falter,
Guide my step, hold my hand all the way.

[1] National Selected Morticians (Evanston, Illinois), A Service Book, p. 178. Used by permission.
[2] © Copyright 1957 Lynn Music Corporation. Used by permission.

125

Assurance from God's Word

"Who shall separate us from the love of Christ? shall tribulation, or distress, or persecution, or famine, or nakedness, or peril, or sword? Nay, in all these things we are more than conquerors through him that loved us. For I am persuaded, that neither death, nor life, nor angels, nor principalities, nor powers, nor things present, nor things to come, nor height, nor depth, nor any other creature, shall be able to separate us from the love of God, which is in Christ Jesus our Lord."   (Rom. 8:35, 37-39)

Committal Statement

O God, our help in ages past, our hope for years to come, into Thy tender care we commit the soul of our beloved————— (name, of brother or sister), thanking Thee for his (her) life and ministry among us, and for the assurance of his (her) abundant entrance into Thy glory. To the ground we commit his (her) body, the earthly house in which he (she) lived, waiting for the day when the glorified body shall be raised from the grave and joined again to his (her) eternal spirit, in that day when "the dead shall hear the voice of the Son of God: and they that hear shall live."

Benediction

"Now unto him that is able to keep you from falling, and to present you faultless before the presence of his glory with exceeding joy, to the only

wise God our Saviour, be glory and majesty, dominion and power, both now and ever. Amen."

(Jude 24, 25)

—*Raymond P. Murray*

BURIAL SERVICE

FOR A CHILD

COMFORT FROM GOD'S WORD

"Wherefore are they before the throne of God, and serve him day and night in his temple: and he that sitteth on the throne shall dwell among them. They shall hunger no more, neither thirst any more; neither shall the sun light on them, nor any heat. For the Lamb which is in the midst of the throne shall feed them, and shall lead them unto living fountains of waters: and God shall wipe away all tears from their eyes." (Rev. 7:15-17)

COMMITTAL STATEMENT

Heavenly Father, whose face the angels of little children do always behold, and who by Thy Son Jesus Christ has taught us that of such is the kingdom of heaven; we commend to Thy keeping the soul of this little child whom Thou hast gathered with the lambs to Thy bosom; and we commit to the bosom of mother earth the body which he (she) lived, [earth to earth, ashes to ashes, dust to dust,][1] looking for the resurrection of the dead, and life everlasting through our Lord Jesus Christ. Amen.

BENEDICTION

"Grace and peace be multiplied unto you through the knowledge of God, and of Jesus our Lord."
(2 Peter 1:2)
—William E. Pickthorn

---

[1] The section enclosed in brackets may be omitted if it seems more appropriate to do so.

BURIAL SERVICE

FOR A NON-CHRISTIAN

COMFORT FROM GOD'S WORD

"Lord, thou hast been our dwelling place in all generations. Before the mountains were brought forth, or ever thou hadst formed the earth and the world, even from everlasting to everlasting, thou art God." (Ps. 90:1, 2)

COMMITTAL STATEMENT

Once again we have been summoned to this city of the dead to lay at rest the mortal remains of one who for a time lived among us as neighbor, loved one, and friend. Memory is hallowed here; for the stones and monuments around us speak of the affection of surviving relatives and friends. Rest is suggested here by the quiet surroundings in which the inhabitants of this city lie. Life beyond the grave is suggested by the renewal from year to year of the flowers and trees and shrubs which, having appeared to die, spring forth into newness of life. That a part of man never dies is the positive affirmation of Christian faith and a declaration of the Holy Bible. This future we leave in the hands of God who is perfect in love, infinite in mercy, and who doeth all things well.

BENEDICTION

"Now God himself and our Father, and our Lord Jesus Christ, direct our way unto you. And the Lord make you to increase and abound in love one toward

129

another, and toward all men, even as we do toward you; to the end he may stablish your hearts unblameable in holiness before God, even our Father, at the coming of our Lord Jesus Christ with all his saints." (1 Thess. 3:11-13)

—William E. Pickthorn